UNBOUNDED WEALTH

12 Simple Steps to Break Free of "The Man" and Live Life on Your Own Terms

JOHN DEL VECCHIO

ILLUSTRATIONS BY JOHN GROH

Charles Street Research

**819 N. CHARLES STREET
BALTIMORE, MD 21201**

ISBN: 978-0-578-53312-4

Copyright © 2019 Charles Street Research. All international and domestic rights reserved, protected by copyright laws of the United States and international treaties. No part of this publication may be reproduced in any form, printed or electronic or on the worldwide web, without written permission from the publisher, Charles Street Research, 819 N. Charles Street, Baltimore, MD 21201.

Notice: This publication is designed to provide accurate and authoritative information in regard to the subject matter covered. It is sold and distributed with the understanding that the author, publisher and seller are not engaged in rendering legal, accounting or other professional advice or service. If legal or other expert assistance is required, the services of a competent professional advisor should be sought.

The information and recommendations contained herein have been compiled from sources considered reliable. Employees, officers and directors of Charles Street Research do not receive fees or commissions for any recommendations of services or products in this book. Investments and other recommendations carry inherent risks. As no investment recommendation can be guaranteed, Charles Street Research takes no responsibility for any loss or inconvenience if one chooses to accept them.

Table of Contents

"Who Am I? Why Am I Here?" 10

Don't Keep Up with the Joneses.
They're Broke. 19

How to Chew Bubblegum and Save
for Retirement at the Same Time 31

Kill Your Debt (Before It Kills You!) 45

The World's Richest Gym Teacher 57

The George Costanza School of Investing. 67

No News Is the Best News for Your Money 79

Double Your Retirement in 5 Minutes 91

Every Stock Has a Middle Name: Danger 103

The World's Scariest Roller Coaster:
No Ticket Required! 114

An Hour Without Oprah 126

Unbounded Wealth and
the Sonic Jubulator 135

The Show Me The Money Strategy to
Crushing the Market in Minutes a Month 148

Other Works from John Del Vecchio 165

ABOUT THE AUTHOR

John Del Vecchio is a forensic accountant at heart. Standing on the shoulders of the great David Tice, James O'Shaughnessy, and Dr. Howard Schilit, he built a framework of algorithms and multi-factor grading systems that have been used in portfolios that have managed several hundred million dollars. He's consulted for billion-dollar asset managers and co-founded one of the original actively managed ETFs on the New York Stock Exchange.

John is the co-author of *Rule of 72: How to Compound Your Money and Uncover Hidden Stock Profits* and *What's Behind the Numbers: A Guide To Exposing Financial Chicanery and Avoiding Huge Losses in Your Portfolio*. He has appeared in *The Wall Street Journal, Barron's, Investor's Business Daily,* and *Fortune*, and on CNBC, Fox, and Bloomberg.

In his free time, John likes to travel, ski, golf, and cook gourmet meals at home.

For Sandy.

You always lived life on your own
terms. May you rest in peace.

PRAISE FOR JOHN DELVECCHIO

- "At Crazy Eddie, we succeeded in perpetrating our financial fraud for many years because most Wall Street analysts and investors took for granted the integrity of our reported numbers. *What's Behind the Numbers?* teaches investors to critically look under the surface and spot red flags that could help them avoid potential losses from fraudulent companies like Crazy Eddie."

  – Sam E. Antar, former Crazy Eddie CFO and convicted felon

- "Wow! A must-read for anyone who thinks they know how to make money in the stock markets! Del Vecchio and Jacobs forced me to confront the stark reality of *What's Behind the Numbers?* It isn't pretty. . . . One of the best books on investing I have read in years."

  – Tom Meredith, venture capitalist, former CFO, of Dell Inc.

- "In the busy world of finance, we don't often have time to read every book that comes out. If you read only one book this year make it this one."

  – Nick G.

- "With so much misinformation out there about investing, it's refreshing to come across an investing book filled with common sense."

  – Todd W.

ACKNOWLEDGEMENTS

I'd like to thank the illustrator for this book, John Groh, for the fun illustrations, and for helping to lighten up a technical topic such as saving and investing.

I'd also like to thank my publisher Shannon Sands for greenlighting this project and my editors, Chase Hoffberger and David Dittman, for making me come across as a much better writer. And Megan Johnson and Andrew McCord from Charles Street Research for their support on the concept and for helping to push the project to completion.

Introduction

Who Am I? Why Am I Here?

Had there been back in 1992 what today we refer to as "memes," that quote from Admiral James Stockdale, introducing himself at a vice presidential debate, would have blown up the internet.

It was awkward. It was funny. It was meme-worthy.

And it's a great way to start our journey together.

So, who am I? And why am I here?

I'm just like you. I have dreams and aspirations. I have things I'd like to accomplish and places I'd like to see. I want a few extra bucks in my pocket to feel more financially secure. I want my money to work for me so that I have the time to do what I want to do. I want freedom. Freedom from "The Man."

Mostly, I want to help other people break free, too. People just like you.

My vision of "breaking free" doesn't include lounging on a yacht sipping fancy champagne from a crystal flute. And there are no "get rich quick" schemes. However, there are plenty of ways to live a better life. And, in my experience, a solid financial footing is the best foundation for a positive, self-sustaining feedback loop.

I'm able to live life on my own terms. *Unbounded Wealth* is my process for doing it. It's become a habit for me – I need to live life on my own terms.

I'm going to help you get to that level, too – good habits breeding good habits – by turning it into a simple, customizable blueprint for action.

But you must choose to do it.

That need to live life on my own terms means I'm totally unemployable by any big corporation or company with a complex organizational chart.

For my first corporate job, I had to wear a suit every day. It wasn't so bad. As the great philosopher Deion Sanders once said, "If you look good, you feel good. If you feel good, you play good. If you play good, you get paid good."

The problem was that the company had a huge employee manual full of all sort of rules. My first official act in my first career job was to throw that employee manual in the trash.

Look, I won't be getting another job at a Fortune 500 company anytime soon. I won't be seeking a job at a Fortune 500 company anytime soon, either. Come to think of it, I don't even think I have a current résumé…

But I do know where I'd start if I had to put one together.

Of course, at this stage, I know enough about job-seeking in the 21st century that someone with my real-world experience shouldn't begin with "Education."

But bear with me as I share a story about my first assignment in college.

My professor was an established business man. He sold his company to Admiral Stockdale's running mate, a guy named Ross Perot, the famous billionaire. It's great to learn from business people because they've actually done it in the real world. It's not an experiment.

Anyway, we were tasked with a four-page case study. During the first class, following the one where we submitted our work on that first assignment, my professor blasted everyone in the room. Let's just say he wasn't very impressed by the quality of work.

I was mortified. It's not the best way to start off your college career. I mean, you're paying to be there. You might as well get a return on your investment.

So, I scheduled a visit during his office hours to get my grade and to review my work. Turns out, I scored a 96, the highest in the class. He told me my work was "graduate level." I'd only been in college a week.

We chatted a bit, and he shared some things about his experience that later proved out in my own. He'd graduated first in his college class. After about two years in the real world, no one cared what his GPA had been or where he'd gone to school.

It was about results. It was about doing good work.

Same thing happened to me. I graduated with honors and a perfect GPA. Certainly, that opened some doors early on, and I got various jobs working with some heavyweights in the financial services industry.

And I got results.

I co-founded an innovative investment product traded on the New York Stock Exchange. I consulted for multi-billion dollar investment funds. Formulas I created are still used on Wall Street by funds that manage nearly $800 million in assets.

Now, that gets me to where I'd start if I were putting together a résumé...

My most important job was as a dishwasher. It's hard work. Standing on my feet was back-breaking at times. It is indeed hot in the kitchen. That's especially so when steam is blowing in your face on an almost constant basis. I was soaked in sweat. There was another dishwasher working with me. He was 43.

I worked my ass off and became a damn good dishwasher. That was the best job I had because I learned I didn't want to be doing it at 43. There was no bigger motivation in the world.

Today, I'm 43. And I've done a lot of interesting work.

In the end, none of it matters. Some of my experiences have helped initially with my path in life. But I would have found a "right" path anyway. I didn't need that specific experience to point me in the right direction. You don't either.

Except the dishwashing...

If fancy degrees, high-paying jobs, or genius IQs were the answer to financial freedom and living life on your own terms, most people wouldn't be broke. We'd all be on the beach sipping Bahama Mamas, watching our brokerage account balances tick higher every few hours.

I'll warn you: A lot of what you're about to read will seem basic – obvious even.

If you find yourself nodding along, repeating to yourself, "I know that," or "no kidding," then you're on the right track. Indeed, the very first thing you might've already noticed about this book is that it's thin. That's because there's no junk in it.

It's not whether you know this stuff. *It's whether you act on it and do it.*

You see, most people think success in this regard is due to some big secret.

So, what's the big secret about breaking free of "The Man?" Come closer, I'll whisper it in your ear…

The big secret is that there is no big secret.

It's all about mastering the basics. *And then doing it.*

"Basic" sometimes gets a bad rap. But I'm reminded of a wonderful story from John Madden, the Super Bowl-winning head coach of the Oakland Raiders who made probably greater fame as the best color commentator in National Football League history.

Years ago, while he was still toiling away at a junior college, he saw that the great Vince Lombardi of the Green Bay Packers was giving a seminar on coaching.

Madden admired Lombardi, thought of him as an idol. So, he emptied his bank account and attended the conference. Madden thought he already knew everything there was to know about coaching, so he played it cool, maybe even a bit too cool. As he put it, he "sat in the back. This is how stupid I was. It's like I was sitting in the back of church."

Lombardi spent the first four hours of the seminar talking about one play, the Power Sweep.

Just one play!

Then they broke for lunch.

After lunch, Lombardi came back and spent another four hours talking about one play – the Power Sweep!

After eight hours of talk about one type of play, Madden left thinking he didn't know a darn thing about football.

Here's the thing: From the outside, the Power Sweep looks basic. And it is – if your team knows how to block. But there are many variables that inform the way an offensive player performs his assigned role, the details of which can cause the play to develop in almost any number of ways, positive and negative.

At the same time, those opposite Lombardi's Packers had to master the basics of tackling to defend against his precise execution.

That's how I think of investing.

In fact, my working title for the investment strategy I outline in Chapter 11 was "The Power Sweep." There are many twists and turns in life, unpredictable events that shape progress. Nothing unfolds in a straight line.

But if you nail down basic blocking skills and tackling techniques, you have a solid foundation. You'll also be way ahead of most people... *way* ahead!

I often wish I was a rocket scientist/astrophysicist/stock-picker capable of conjuring complex theories NASA would use to solve humankind's greatest mysteries while conquering financial markets on the side.

But I'm not. And I'm content with who I am. My views are basic. I've taken a lot of time and conscious effort to develop a set of habits around them that've helped me get to a place where I feel free from "The Man."

If you're reading this book, perhaps you're seeking a similar path.

The good news is human nature is predictable. Change is possible, but only through time and effort. But it doesn't require a lot of extra brainpower to find your own freedom.

Learning these basics will help you, too.

This is the first time I've taken on the task of writing a book as a solo project. I am a co-author of two other books. The first – *What's Behind the Numbers?* – was published by McGraw-Hill in 2012. It was a big deal for me. When I was a kid, I was a slow reader. In third grade, I was in remedial English.

Back then, the world was not very politically correct. Kids weren't coddled. There were no awards for participating. So, my parents were told I wouldn't amount to much.

Years later, I was published by a major house. *What's Behind the Numbers?* went on to win awards, including the Stock Trader's Almanac Book of the Year for 2013. It was praised in *Barron's*. My alma mater recognized me as a "distinguished alumnus."

Those honors were – and still are – nice. But there's a problem with *What's Behind the Numbers?*

The problem with the book is that it was written in too technical a way for it to be broadly consumed. Sure, it does well with grad students and Wall Street types. It's on college syllabi, and firms have bought it in bulk to distribute to clients. I've spoken at places like Google, in front of major investor groups, and to big insurance companies.

But then there's someone like my dad. He read it… at least, he tried to. He told me he was very proud of me and that he got through 30 pages and didn't understand a darn thing I said. My mother felt the same way. Now, if you ever want confirmation of my greatness, just talk with my Mom.

I want to write something anyone can understand. I want to write a book that can help people establish and walk a right financial path for them, one that gets them a life they want.

That's what I call *Unbounded Wealth*.

Here are the three rules I set out for the project:

- It's short. You should be able to be read this book in the time it takes to fly from Chicago to Dallas. We're all pressed for time, so I made this read short and sweet. There are plenty of long and fascinating (and also boring) investment books out there. The internet is littered with them.

- It's "easy and breezy." We're having a conversation about easily digestible concepts. You won't need a highlighter to help you remember details. I'm not boosting egos with fancy words. *Unbounded Wealth* is about getting you on a path to freedom, starting with your finances.

- It's illustrated. I'm told pictures are worth a lot of words. Including a few sounds efficient to me, so we've included some illustrations to reinforce the lessons we talk about. They're fun, they're informative, and they break up the reading.

There you have it.

"Basic blocking and tackling" is the foundation. If you embrace the following concepts, you'll be well on the way to establishing financial security and living your life on your own terms.

Chapter 1

Don't Keep Up with the Joneses. They're Broke.

"Before you try to keep up with the Joneses, be sure they're not trying to keep up with you." – Erma Bombeck

Achieving unbounded wealth is a function of having the right mindset. Now, do you have "the right mindset?" Let's start by observing what others are doing. What better place to start than with what we're often told is the ideal American family.

You may have heard the phrase "keeping up with the Joneses." That's a shorthand expression to set up a comparison between you and other folks, including your friends and neighbors. It's about social standing – and it's about the accumulation of material goods.

So, let's call our "ideal" American family the Joneses. And let's see if it adds up.

The Dream

Who are the Joneses, specifically?

They're perfect. They're "living the dream" sold by advertisers and even the government as the one we should all strive to create.

They own a McMansion. They own at least two cars, and at least one of them is very big and consumes a lot of gas. They own five flat-panel TVs, several computers, multiple handheld devices. Mrs. Jones has a very large diamond on her ring finger. Mr. Jones owns the latest space-age golf clubs, the set that automatically corrects your slice so you can avoid the driving range and stroll onto the first tee like you're Arnold Palmer.

The kids have perfect hair and teeth. They have all the latest tech gadgets. They take piano lessons… dance lessons… Sanskrit lessons. They play travel soccer and travel hockey and swim year-round. There's zero down time.

Then there's the staff. Managing that McMansion and all those busy schedules requires staff. There's the cleaning lady, pool guy, and the yard crew. Together, the staff keeps the Joneses house looking bright and shiny.

From the outside looking in, the Joneses have it all. They *are* the American Dream. The more they make, the more they spend. Life's good with all those TVs, cars, and golf clubs.

There's a problem with this picture, though. It's a farcical charade.

The truth is, the Joneses are broke.

It wasn't always this way. In 1975, the year I was born, the average house was about 1,645 square feet. Recent data from the U.S. Census Bureau show that in 2017 the average size of a completed single-family house was 2,631 square feet.

A typical family consisted of about 2.94 people way back in 1975. Today, it's about 2.54.

All that extra square footage is surely required to satisfy this 21st century fascination with self-gratification and personal space.

My grandparents owned one car. They never moved into a bigger house when the size of their family went from two to five. My mom and her siblings shared rooms. They spent time together playing games and watching the TV. They had diversions like running, chasing, hiding, tagging, and getting lost.

Hard today for zombified kids to get lost… or to find themselves.

They were never rich, but my grandparents were able to fund their modest middle-class lifestyle in their later years. They also had enough for elderly care when it came to that point. And they still enjoyed life and spent money on things that made them happy. It was mostly about experiences.

That's my "get off my lawn" rant. And it undoubtedly reflects my own biases. But it does illustrate in stark terms a basic reality.

The Reality

So, what happened from then until now? Yes, times have changed. Let's think big, broad picture, with both irony and low-level but persistent tragedy...

The short answer – and the problem *Unbounded Wealth* addresses – is that as society has evolved, the financial situation of the typical American family has worsened.

It's actually quite sad, the real financial state of the Joneses. This does not have to be you. But, before we can get to where we're going, we need to understand where we are today.

Let's take a look at the financial state of the average American.

Let's start with savings. The typical American family has less than $60,000 in investment savings. That amount of money won't go very far if something happens to the breadwinners in the Jones family. It's impossible to maintain that lifestyle with such a low level of savings.

The Joneses can only hope there's no "rainy day," ever.

Unfortunately, the risk of a rainy day is much higher than typically contemplated by the average American. The Joneses are simply unprepared.

Beyond the unpredictable life events that inevitably crop up, there's *no chance* of retirement for the Joneses. You can forget the idea of a waterfront retreat where you'll watch the sun set. That money would be blown through in a heartbeat.

The reality is the Joneses live to work. They're completely at the mercy of "The Man." Any false moves, their world falls apart, fast.

The numbers get worse when you slice and dice them a little more finely. Consider Baby Boomers, a generation of nearly 80 million folks.

People, on average, have just $136,000 socked away for retirement. Each day, 10,000 more of them hit 65, the age of Social Security retirement. It's like a herd of cattle running to the edge of a cliff. They haven't gone over yet, so we haven't seen specific consequences. But it is going to be awful.

What's scarier is that Baby Boomers enjoyed their peak earning years during a historic bull market for stocks. Where did all that money go?

Shockingly, according to surveys conducted by BankRate.com, nearly half of Americans are unable to fund an emergency expense of as little as $400 if one were to pop up.

It's true that 20% of American families also make more than $100,000 a year. That seems like a lot of money. Actually… it is a lot of money! The bad news is that, according to a 2015 Nielsen study, 25% of families making $150,000 a year or more live paycheck to paycheck.

That's crazy!

Is Enough Ever Enough?

So, where does it all go?! The answer is, it becomes your "stuff."

We're weighed down by "stuff." It consumes us. The average American household has over 300,000 things.

Three. Hundred. Thousand. *Things!*

It has become such a problem that there are TV shows about it. People watch other people hoard all their junk while they sit on their sofa and stuff over-processed foods down their throats.

In the 21st century, the average household income has been mostly flat. But we continue to buy, buy, buy… and that's making us indentured servants to "The Man." That's the only way we can feed our addiction to "stuff."

Breaking free and having unbounded wealth is not *easy*. But it is *simple*.

Let's focus right now on the simple part. One of the most important rules is to ditch the consumption culture we encounter day-to-day in the First World. Leave it behind. Don't look back.

George Carlin is one of my favorite comedians. He was wonderfully observant, and he could inject belly-breaking humor into serious and important topics. He summed up the consumption culture we live in better than anyone:

Consumption. This is the new national pastime. F**k baseball. It's consumption, the only true, lasting American Value that's left…buying things…People spending money they don't have on things they don't need…so they can max out their credit cards

People these days have too many things.

and spend the rest of their lives paying 18 percent interest on something that cost $12.50. And they didn't like it when they got home anyway. Not too bright, folks, not too f****n' bright.

It's easy to get sucked in by the consumption culture. In the "always on, constantly connected" age we're bombarded with advertisements 24 hours a day, seven days a week. We're exposed to 4,000 to 10,000 advertisements per day. Politicians encourage us to shop as an act of "patriotism."

So, we buy, buy, buy…

And it's become an addiction.

Consider this simple equation:

**Money Coming In – Money Going Out =
Money Left to Break Free of The Man**

To break the vicious cycle that's sucking money out of your wallet and making you a slave, first take a deep breath and slow down.

Look at each and every purchase. Is it absolutely necessary? Does it improve the quality of your life?

Or did you fritter away $6 on a triple espresso latte milkshake? Are you wasting your money and your health? Look, I've been there. The only shame is not making a new, better habit.

Before you achieve unbounded wealth, you must take stock of your behavior. You must monitor your spending habits. Then, you must build a nest egg through consistent investment.

Maybe you don't make $100,000. Maybe your income is below average. But, even if that's the case, you can still build wealth. This is a legitimate and serious issue. So, we'll tackle it throughout this book.

Just $2 a day saved at 21 years old at 7% annualized interest grows to over $208,000 by the time you're 65. And that's beaucoup bucks compared with the average savings held by today's Baby Boomer!

Start keeping track of where you spend your money. Those $6 Frappucinos all add up.

That's not to say you can't splurge. But, if you're not saving any money, you need to identify where it's going. Money is getting wasted somewhere. You need to find out where… and then plug that leaky hole.

The consumption economy is literally killing us, individually and as a society. We need to change our behavior.

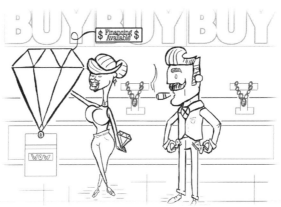

Your life will be easier if you don't worry as often about what you plan to buy next.

Ditch it now. Take control of your life.

Here's my mindset. I don't give two hoots what other people have. In fact, I'm genuinely happy for people inside my circle of life if they have success. There's not an envious bone in my body. I have friends that make minimum wage. I have friends that own private jets.

That mindset eliminates a lot of baggage. Since I don't care what other people have, I'm not weighed down by any social pressures to keep up. Those pressures are only getting worse with the explosion in social media and the proliferation of "influencers."

"Influencers" often show off dramatically – sometimes even criminally – unrealistic lifestyles. Much, if not all of it, is smoke and mirrors. That doesn't mean, however, that it can't create real problems in society, such as anxiety and depression.

Don't get me wrong: I like nice things, too. I like to dress well, for example. If you run into me at the airport, it's unlikely you'll find me in loungewear and flip-flops looking like I just rolled out of bed and into the terminal.

But I don't overbuy. I also take care of business first by following the other rules of unbounded wealth I'll discuss throughout this book.

Also, as my own success fluctuates, I don't change my habits. I bought my first home just after I turned 27. It was the least expensive condo in the nicest neighborhood. The developer needed to get a lien off the property by Tuesday. I walked in on Saturday.

I was able to negotiate a much better "finish out," with improved upgrades at no additional cost, because he needed a contract signed ASAP. I didn't "need" it. I didn't even let the seller know I wanted it.

Initially, it was a bit of a stretch for me financially. But I knew I was getting a big raise a month later and a bonus six months after that. Over time, my income grew. But I resisted the urge to "trade up" for a bigger, "better" place.

Instead, I paid off the mortgage in 11 years while also funding my retirement along the way and spending money on great experiences. I could have sold the place, moved into a fancier shell, and turned it into a glorified sinkhole. To impress…?

I was already in a beautiful place. I was happy. I was what we believe the Joneses to be: free.

It worked out well because when I finally decided to sell the place, it went in less than 48 hours, for cash, at the highest price per square foot that any unit had ever sold in the building. Had I moved up to the super deluxe apartment in the sky, I might still be trying to sell it!

Still, I get sucked into advertisements, just like the rest of us. I have biases, desires, and pleasures. I love to cook. I'd much rather cook at home than eat out at a restaurant. I also invested in a nice kitchen with professional appliances. I get value from them because I use them.

Not long ago, I saw an advertisement for an oven-like machine that uses light rays to perfectly sear a steak and cook other tasty foods in just a few minutes. I love a juicy, perfectly cooked steak.

The machine was sleek. It was cutting-edge. It would have looked sweet on my countertop. It would have upped my game in the meat department. There was a lot of appeal to own that oven.

Yes... this device grabbed my attention, like a kid in a candy store. But I fell back on my rules. And one of the big ones is "don't buy anything without a cooling-off period." I usually wait at least 72 hours. And I typically don't pay full price for anything.

Fortunately, I also had a professional chef who follows me on LinkedIn. I asked his advice, and he calmly walked me off the ledge... and saved me $1,200!

The next time you open your wallet and whip out your credit card to pay for some trinket, interrogate yourself:

- Is it worth what I'm paying?
- How often will I use it?
- How else can I use this money?
- How long did I have to work to earn the money to pay for it?
- Will it make me happy?
- Why am I paying with a credit card?
- If I pay for it myself instead of buying it with borrowed money, how much better off will I be?

During my 72-hour cooling off period, I think about these questions. My impulse purchases are zero. And, while I do splurge from time to time, I've put some thought into it rather than be carried away by emotion.

One less dollar paid in interest to the credit card company is one more dollar I have for ME!

When we accumulate more ME dollars, we can invest them and grow our pile. Over time, we're less reliant on others to dictate the course of our lives. We control our time.

That's true freedom.

That's unbounded wealth.

Chapter 2
How to Chew Bubblegum and Save for Retirement at the Same Time

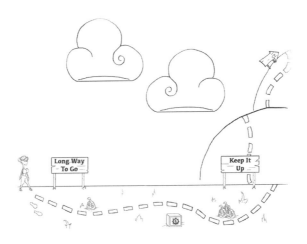

"A journey of a thousand miles begins with a single step." – Laozi

A journey of a thousand miles begins with a single step. That's the best way to think about financial freedom. It's a journey. It may take a while. It'll most likely take longer than you'd like. There are no "get rich quick" schemes.

When you think about retiring, imagining your life 30 or 40 years from now, or making life a little better in the immediate future, it may seem like a long way off. It may seem impossible.

It's easy to feel overwhelmed. There's a lot to do between "now" and "then," and so much time. And, because it seems so far off, it's *easy* to put it off for another day.

But those days add up.

Instead of delaying, if you focus on the here and now and work in bite-sized chunks, you'll reach your destination. Slowly. But the journey will be far less overwhelming.

I often think about the time when I moved to Dallas. Still seems like yesterday. It was more than 17 years ago! Time flies, and it stops for no one.

I've come a long way since then. Back then, I had left what little I had behind in Alexandria, Virginia, to start fresh. I hopped in the car with whatever would fit in my trunk and drove across the country. I ended up in a crappy apartment with nothing more than a new mattress on the floor and a sofa. No TV, no internet, no fridge, no food… no nothing.

A lot's happened in my life since then. But those 17 years really flew by. Another 17 years from now, I'll be 60 years old!

"Thirty years on" gets here faster than you think it will, a lot faster. That makes it hard to focus. That's a problem. Whatever we might be doing, wherever we might be going, we need to bring it back to a single step and take one at a time.

Take Good Time

There's a good lesson to be learned from the world of professional golf.

The first thing you'll notice is that a professional golfer has a consistent routine. They don't just step up to the ball and whack away. That's what amateurs who never get any better do. They just go to the driving range and blast away as hard as they can. And they wonder why they never improve.

Professionals use a routine to achieve consistency. They may stand behind the ball and envision the shot they're trying to hit. Then, they'll step to the ball from the side and take their stance. Maybe they'll look at the target one more time before they start their swing.

By taking the same steps over and over in the same order, they establish consistent results from shot to shot. They don't always hit a perfect shot. But their routine puts them in the best position to do so on any given swing, swing after swing, round after round, tournament after tournament.

The second thing a professional golfer does is takes it one shot at a time.

Yes, it's a cliché. Listen to a pro conduct an interview on TV. They almost always talk about playing "one shot at a time." This is especially true if they're in the lead with 18 holes to play on Sunday. They say this so they don't get ahead of themselves.

If they're on the sixth hole and they know the ninth is going to be a total grind just to make par, they aren't thinking ahead to the ninth hole. They know they have to play the ninth. But there's also eight and seven. And they're still on six.

The play is to take one shot at a time.

That tells me that a pro golfer, facing tons of pressure and big money-making opportunity, doesn't want to get ahead of himself. When you get ahead of yourself, scary thoughts creep into your head.

Those scary thoughts might work against you in the moment. Take things one step at a time and you'll be much better off.

Watching a professional basketball player shoot a free throw is another good example of the cumulative benefits of "routine." The very best follow the same steps over and over again. They set their feet, eye their target at the front or the back of the rim, close their eyes, dribble the ball twice, spin it in their hands, and then – and only then – take the shot.

By doing the same thing over and over again, they establish an expectation of similar results. They don't change the way they set their feet. They don't change their target from the front to the back of the rim, or vice versa; they don't vary the number of times they dribble the ball.

They don't shoot right-handed one time, left-handed the next.

They do the same thing, over and over again.

To achieve our dreams, we need to set goals. And we need to take one step at a time in that direction. That's how you achieve consistency and move toward your destination.

Two Simple Steps

Quite simply, quite literally, start with a single step.

That first step is to figure out where you stand today financially. The second step is to set some goals defining where you'd like to be. Even if you're only a few years away from retirement... even if you're retired... goals are good. Goals work.

Let's break it down...

Gather all your records of savings and retirement accounts as well as ongoing expenses like credit card bills, your mortgage statement, and your car payment.

Take a look at the money being drained from your pocket each month. One helpful action you can take is to write down your expenses. Write *everything* down! Track your expenses over the next month just to get in the habit of keeping an eye on where your money's going.

You may think you're broke. But money is flying out the door, probably chasing some bad habit. Did you really need that burger and fries? That new pair of pants... well, maybe, if you're doing that burger-and-fries thing too often. It's a negative feedback loop.

If you identify – in writing – where your money's being spent, you'll be more motivated to take corrective action. I guarantee it. And I guarantee you'll end up with more of it in your pocket at the end of each pay period after you do.

Here's a big one. I just saved about $2,400 annually myself in one simple step. I canceled subscriptions. Most of them were for apps related to streaming services and other online expenses.

The average American thinks they spend $80 per month on subscriptions. Actually, it's about $240. Truth is, I wasn't using that stuff very much. So, when I sat down and looked at it closely, I slashed and burned my way to pretty good savings every month.

I'm sure Jeff Bezos at Amazon.com isn't going to miss the $119 I'm no longer paying for a Prime subscription. But I was getting a little "Amazoned out" anyway, so it was an easy decision to make. So were the others. A couple hundred bucks a month isn't chump change. It's real money.

Expense and Consequence

Little expenses add up over time and eat into your retirement balance. Let's look at three examples.

For the sake of this thought experiment, let's say that over the next 30 years you earn a respectable 7% annually on your retirement account.

The first thing we'll consider is a simple purchase. You want to buy a pack of gum. It's good gum, so it costs $1 per pack. Over 30 years, if you earn 7% annually, that pack of gum will have cost $7.61 out of your future financial independence. It doesn't seem like so much, does it?

On the other hand, we have the flat-panel TV. The newest technology seems to always run in the area of $2,000. Over 30 years, that $2,000 cut a whopping $15,224 from your retirement savings.

Finally, you decide to purchase a new car. That $50,000 ride – with shiny wheels and air-conditioned seats – will set you back the princely sum of $381,000 over 30 years.

Money brings consequences, a reality you cannot escape.

Of course, as soon as you drive it off the lot, it'll lose a third of its value. Plus, it won't even be drivable in 30 years!

Every expense has a consequence.

That's not to say you can't chew gum or drive a nice car. But, if you're not saving for your retirement, and instead spend your time throwing money around without paying close attention to where it's going, those expenses will have serious consequences down the road.

It's popular advice to tell people not to drink a Starbucks coffee every day because that $5 literally adds up to a fortune over time. That's true. The thing is, if Starbucks makes your life better, then go for it! But only do so if you're already taking care of all the other things you need to do to set yourself up for a better future.

Sadly, most people don't do the right things, and that Starbucks expense does indeed end up as wasted money.

There are people who take managing expenses and cutting back to extremes. Consider the case of Michelle McGagh.

Ms. McGagh is a financial journalist from London. She decided to buy nothing new for an entire year. She still had to spend money on basics, like her mortgage and insurance. Food costs likely went way down, as she spent $45 a week. Everything else was slashed without mercy. No restaurant meals, no beers at the local pub, no gym membership, no fancy shoes, and no candy bars.

The result? Ms. McGagh saved about $27,000 over the course of a year. This helped her reduce her mortgage substantially. She also learned that she was much happier living a simpler life and not bogged down by accumulating possessions.

The Magic Formula

We don't have to cut out all spending on life's little luxuries.

But, before we can set goals to achieve financial freedom, we have to know and abide by the Magic Formula.

The Magic Formula is very simple. But it's not always easy to get a positive result. Fortunately, no advanced algebra or trigonometry is required! Here it is:

Income – Expenses = Excess Cash

No matter what you do, you *must* spend less than you make in income. There's no way around this fact.

If you're living paycheck to paycheck, getting the Magic Formula to yield you a positive number could lead to some hard choices.

Think about how much money you'd have if you didn't buy that coffee every morning.

Did you discover in your daily tracking of expenses that the frothy cup of coffee at the local brew house is costing you $150 a month?! Well, it might be time to make your cup of wake-me-up at home, where it costs less than $0.05 a serving.

Are those four pairs of pants you bought at that most recent "sale of a lifetime" gathering dust in your closet? It might be time to donate them to charity for a tax deduction. But, please, do not replace them. According to the chief designer of California Closets, the average person uses only 20% of their wardrobe anyway.

Are you not getting use out of that $250-per-month gym membership? Might be time to cancel. Packing on a few extra pounds because you're eating out three days a week? That's a very fast way to drain your wallet. Eating out is expensive. Learning to cook might have other benefits beyond just being cheaper. It's also healthier, and you can impress your loved ones.

Get SMART

Now that we know what we spend and we've digested the Magic Formula, we can begin to set goals to reach our retirement destination.

Very simply, our goals will help create a budget for us to live by so that the Magic Formula yields a positive result.

One of the better formats I've seen for setting goals is a system called SMART. Each letter stands for a different goal setting concept:

S = Specific

M = Measurable

A = Agreed

R = Realistic

T = Time-Based

Let's tackle each concept one by one and see how they can help us reach financial independence.

"S" is for Specific: This is self-explanatory. Your goals can't be vague. The more precise they are, the easier they'll be to measure and achieve. Because we're often talking about retiring in the very distant future, I find that both long-term and short-term goals are needed.

Your long-term goal might be, "I want to have a million dollars set aside for retirement in 20 years." Your short-term goal might state, "I want to save an extra $100 this week."

Your goals should work together. As you save $100 this week, you're working toward your longer-term million-dollar goal. An extra C-note in your retirement account might not seem like it'll further your retirement dreams. But, over 20 years at 7% annually, that's $387 added to your bottom line!

Remember, be very precise!

"M" is for Measurable: You must measure your performance as it relates to achieving your goals. The good news here is that we're mostly talking about money. It's easy to quantify and keep track of.

If your goal is to save an extra $100 this week, it'll be easy to measure that. Either you saved $100 or you didn't. Maybe you saved more. Whatever the result, you can now compare your performance to your goals and adjust as time goes on.

You should take measurements along the way to achieving your goal, not just at the end. If your weekly goal is to save $100, it might pay to check in on day three to see where you're at. Maybe all the savings came up front, such as not going out to dinner on Tuesday. Or, maybe it's that sale of the latest trinket you plan to avoid this weekend.

Plan, plan, plan. Measure, measure, measure.

"A" is for Agreed: This is an important one. The other stakeholders in your quest for financial independence have to agree on and buy into the concept. If you're saving an extra $100 this week but your husband blew $250 on a night at the casino, his actions are at odds with your goals.

Everyone needs to be on the same page. And everyone needs to be held accountable. That includes children, spouses, and any other members of the household. That does not include friends and extended family.

Remember, the Joneses are broke. We don't need to worry about what they are or are not doing. We also have to shrug off the peer pressure that comes with being sucked into the consumption culture.

"Buy-in" is critical to your success.

"R" is for Realistic: If you make $1,000 a week but set a goal for saving $2,000, that's unrealistic. By now, you've written down where you're spending money, all of your expenses. The easiest thing to do is work backward.

If you know you're spending $25 a week on expensive coffee beverages but you just can't live without it once or twice a week, you can at least find $15 to $20 in weekly savings. Not buying a pair of pants or a dress just because it's on sale might yield another $50 to $75. Turning the heat down a few degrees and wearing a sweater might save you $3 that week.

Knowing your expenses and taking action to contain them will help you achieve realistic goals. The great thing is, once you start to have some success from week to week, you'll build confidence. And that confidence will lead to more success. It's a positive feedback loop. You'll quickly start to feel much better about yourself.

"T" is for Time: Goals are nothing without deadlines. Don't set open-ended aims, such as, "I want to have a million dollars when I retire." Set a specific date.

The lack of a deadline makes it impossible to track your progress. It can also cause you to be lazy and push off until a later date that which can easily be done today. Everything is easier to handle in the here and now.

Once we've set some SMART goals, we can take corrective action if we stray off course. Don't get down if you miss a short-term goal or two. Take stock of your situation and work even harder to jump those hurdles the next week or the next month.

The last step we need to take is to act consistently.

The best performers in life approach their craft consistently. For example, watch a professional golfer work their way around a course. The very best will have the exact same routine for every drive, approach shot, and putt throughout the 18 holes.

To be sure, she won't hit every drive right down the middle of the fairway. There will be unforced errors. But consistency of process will allow her to regain her focus and to execute the shot at hand without getting bogged down by the poor shot that's in the past.

If you set goals, consistently apply them, and use corrective action where needed, you, too, can achieve your dreams.

Chapter 3
Kill Your Debt (Before It Kills You!)

"Things which matter most must never be at the mercy of things which matter least." – Johann Wolfgang von Goethe

Earlier we studied the Magic Formula. That name, of course, only makes it sound fancy and mysterious. Because it isn't. It is super-duper simple. And it's the key to not only breaking free of "The Man," but of the kingdom, too.

The Magic Formula states the following:

Income – Expenses = Excess Cash

This is the biggest No Matter What that you'll find in this book: You must spend less than you take in. This is the only way to create excess cash that we use to save and invest and shore up your future.

There are a few ways to generate excess cash. You can earn more income. You can reduce your expenses. Or, you can do both. So far, we've talked about ditching the consumption culture and tracking our expenses. The goal is to identify what's wasteful so it can be cut.

In the next chapter, we'll talk about generating more income.

Right now, let's focus on the flexibility we create simply by taking care of the expense piece of the equation. If our income stays the same but we cut expenses, we increase our cash flow.

Any increase in cash flow should be used to *pay yourself first* until you have maxed out those options.

What do I mean by paying yourself first?

I mean taking care of your financial house *before* anything else. **You** come first!

The most important step you can take is to eliminate as much debt as possible as soon as you can.

Only you can grow your own nest egg.

In case you didn't draw your own conclusion based on my last name, I'm Italian. I think it's in my DNA to pay cash for *everything*. I use credit lightly. In the 23 years since I've had a credit card, I haven't paid a cent in interest. Not one penny.

You don't get rich paying someone else 15% a year to buy stuff you don't need with money you don't have.

It's really that simple. I'll say it again:

You don't get rich paying someone else 15% a year to buy stuff you don't need with money you don't have.

For the people in the back…

YOU DON'T GET RICH PAYING SOMEONE ELSE 15% A YEAR TO BUY STUFF YOU DON'T NEED WITH MONEY YOU DON'T HAVE!

Credit card companies aren't your friends. Friends don't charge friends 15% to 20%, or more, to borrow money. And you're never going to get ahead if you're constantly paying the minimum amount due on a monthly credit card bill.

That's not to say you can't use a credit card. If you rent a car, a hotel room, or buy an airplane ticket, you'll need one. They do have uses. But credit cards need to be used carefully.

Same goes for a house.

Why is it good to have a tax deduction for your mortgage interest? Have you ever looked at a mortgage amortization schedule? All of the interest is billed and paid up front. I paid off my first home in 11 years. What's more, I lived in the same place for 15 years, despite years where my income was several times higher than when I first bought it.

I obeyed the Magic Formula.

Just because I made more money didn't mean I needed to blow it. My digs were plenty fine. I was very happy with what I had. I was grateful every day for my situation. There's no need to keep up with the Joneses.

There are plenty of ways to reduce the bite of taxes without paying interest to a bank. If you need a mortgage to buy a reasonable house to put a roof over your head, consider one. The key word is "reasonable."

Think it through before you sign on the dotted line, and don't get in over your head.

Buying a primary residence isn't going to make you rich. And, despite what you might see on TV, neither will flipping houses for big profits. They never show the folks who lose their butts trying to flip a rehab project.

There are no "get rich quick" schemes that don't blow up in the end. And your home shouldn't be a vehicle to make you feel rich. In fact, over time, housing prices go up about as much as inflation.

It won't make you rich. But owning my property outright is a great stress reliever. *I own it.* No one else. That frees me up to do other things with my excess cash flow, like invest in myself.

It'll put you closer to being free of "The Man," too.

Kill Your Debt Before It Kills You!

Reducing and eliminating debt is the most important step in the process toward financial independence.

We've already discussed a couple concepts designed to put you in position to eliminate all debts. Once we're spending less money – or no money – on "stuff" that we don't need and won't make us happier, we can blowtorch our outstanding debts.

It'd be a lie to tell you paying off your debt is painless. It's not. By now, you're likely consumed by consumption. It's the American way!

Forgoing things like the daily $5 cup of coffee won't be easy, at first. But, over time, as you make progress, you'll feel better about yourself. You'll feel better about the process. These good feelings will reinforce your debt-cutting moves.

And it'll happen a lot faster than you think.

One approach is to make it a game. Why can't debt-cutting be a game? One with a wonderful conclusion? You're a guaranteed winner.

Instead of collecting $200 every time you pass "Go" on a Monopoly board, you get independence... independence forever. You get to live on your own terms. It's one of those journeys you have to take to appreciate it. And the terrain can be extremely rewarding.

Makes the destination all the more spectacular.

"Write It All Down"

If you want to eliminate your debt, you first need to know what it is. So, the first step is to make a list of all of them.

Typical debts are mortgages, car payments, credit card bills, credit extended by retailers, medical bills, and anything else that you owe to others that's eating up your paycheck before you can even think about something like paying yourself.

Write it all down. Get organized. This is very important. Chances are you don't know where your cash is flowing, especially if it's all away from you.

Until I started writing things down, I often found myself scratching my head, wondering why I didn't have as much left in the bank as "I should."

Chances are you have a spreadsheet program on one of the computers you own, desktop, laptop, handheld... that may be the best way (perhaps even an ironic one!) to organize your debts.

Blow torching your debt is an easy way to get ahead..

Then, you can add in formulas and sort them much more easily. (You might even Excel your way into a new skillset.)

But an old-fashioned pencil and the back of a napkin will work just as well.

Write it all down. Get organized.

Next, look at your debts and do a little analysis. There are two major numbers that should stick out.

First is the size of the debt. For example, you may owe $10,000 on your car. Next is the interest rate you're paying on that debt. Your car payment may include a 7% (or perhaps even higher) interest rate.

Once you know how much you owe and how much it's costing you each year, you can start to tackle your debts.

List your debts from smallest to largest, in terms of raw dollar amount owed. Then, list them from the highest interest rate to the lowest. Finally, figure out what that interest is costing you each year to hold that debt.

Should you pay off the largest loans first? The highest interest loans?

My answer, like it is for most things in life is that it depends.

If your biggest loan also carries the highest interest rate, it makes sense to tackle that debt aggressively. On the other hand, it may also make sense psychologically to pay off some small loans in the meantime as well.

Here's what I mean. Let's say you have 15 different debts. But five of them are small, and if you work at it, you could pay them off in a year. If you can do that while chipping away at the debts costing you the most money, this combination approach could work wonders.

The next year, you'll have 10 debts. So, you eliminated a third of the debts, from 15 down to 10, while also reducing the highest-cost debts. That money can then be funneled into knocking down the 10 debts that are left. Maybe the next year you have seven debts.

It's that kind of progress on both parts of the equation – reducing the total interest paid and the number of debts outstanding – that makes you feel accomplished.

The burden gets more reasonable, and that creates positive feedback in your debt-elimination journey.

Save It for Now and Later

What do you do when you're free of debt? **Save!**

Sadly, Americans are in debt to the tune of trillions of dollars, but only a small percentage of us save for our futures.

The statistics surrounding retirement investing are troublesome. Even as more and more people are worried about retirement, fewer and fewer workers are socking away cash or even have access to retirement plans.

How we treat tax-deferred accounts just about qualifies as criminal neglect.

In 2013, just 39% of workers had a 401(k) plan. That's down from 50% in 1999. The median value of a 401(k) plan in the U.S. is just over $18,000! The median is the number smack in the middle. According to the Employee Benefit Research Institute, 40% of workers have less than $10,000 saved.

Only about 13% of folks max out their 401(k) contributions. Worse, households with income of more than $100,000 a year aren't much better at saving. Just 40% of those six-figure families are maxing out their 401(k) plans. I'm certain there are areas of waste in their spending. It might not be easy to find. That's why you need to write it down.

According to the Internal Revenue Service, only 8% of taxpayers eligible to contribute to an individual retirement account did so in 2010. That's a crisis, plain and simple. People simply do not have enough money saved, for the present much less the future.

You don't have to be a statistic. Act now, get invested in these plans if they're available to you, and max out your contributions.

Even if you have some debt, it makes sense to plow some cash flow into tax-deferred retirement accounts. Investing in these plans is like getting a free return on your money!

You're probably most familiar with the 401(k) program that's probably offered as a benefit of your employment. Sign up, today.

Currently, you can save $19,000 per year pre-tax in a 401(k) plan. If you're over 50, you can throw in another $6,000 as a "catch up" contribution. If you're in a high tax bracket, this is similar to earning 50-100% immediately on your money since you're not paying tax on that income. Sounds like a pretty good deal to me!

You're not going to make an immediate 100% on your money anywhere else! You can read all the investment books in the world, and you still won't do any better than simply maximizing your pre-tax savings.

If you're in a high tax bracket, that means you likely make ample money to contribute to your 401(k) plan. If you're not maxing it out, you have serious work to do.

Even if you're not in a high tax bracket, it's still pre-tax savings. Would you rather have the money, or would you rather hand it over to the government?

In addition to pre-tax savings, many employers match retirement contributions up to a certain level. They may match 50% of the first 6% of your salary contributed to the 401(k) plan. This is free money! It's easier to earn than asking for a raise.

Even if you can't max out your 401(k) contribution, kick in at least enough take advantage of the "employer match."

Plowing your hard-earned dough into the "pay yourself first" project will make a huge difference in your pot of gold, and it'll get you closer to freedom.

If your employer doesn't offer a 401(k) program, you can set one up if you own your own business, even a side business. It's easy to do, and it doesn't cost a penny.

Regardless of your 401(k) situation, you can set up an Individual Retirement Account and save $5,500 a year if you're under 50 and an extra $1,000 a year if you're older than 50.

Depending on your income level, these contributions may be tax-deductible. Or, you may qualify for a Roth IRA, which is an after-tax contribution that then grows on a tax-free basis.

There are other options for small-business owners, such as profit-sharing plans and defined benefit plans.

There are plenty of other retirement plans out there. Here's a summary check-list to get you started on your personal investigation:

- 401(k) Plan – Check with your employer.
- Roth IRA – Check with your financial institution to see if you qualify. This is also easy to research on the internet.
- Traditional IRA – Check with your accountant, or research online about getting a tax deduction.
- Profit-sharing plans and defined benefit plans – If you own your own business, research these retirement options as well.

This alphanumeric soup might create some confusion at first. I imagine your mind will sharpen as you begin to focus on how much you can do with them.

There's plenty of information available on the internet. And most online interfaces make it simple to open accounts and set them up based on your scenario.

Just a 401(k) and an IRA, though, offer the opportunity to save *tens of thousands of dollars per year*. And they reduce your tax bill, too. The earlier you start, the better. But it's never too late to get started. Even late-blooming savers can do it effectively.

Not taking advantage of these options – at any stage – is literally flushing money down the toilet.

Chapter 4
The World's Richest Gym Teacher

"The most important investment you can make is in yourself."
– Warren Buffett

Time is the most valuable asset. No matter how successful we are, we all run out of it. Our most valuable cash-producing asset is ourselves. If we can maximize our own abilities, we can increase our cash flow and maximize the time that we have at our disposal.

Time to do what we want is freedom. Freedom from "The Man" is unbounded wealth.

Now that you're scaling back your consumption habits, paying down debt, and maximizing tax-efficient retirement plans, you're well ahead of the Joneses. From here you can turn it up a notch, take a significant leap forward, and invest in yourself.

Warren Buffet's advice in the chapter-opening epigraph is spot-on. I'm living proof. My highest returns and biggest payoffs have come by investing in myself.

I've never lost money making bets on yours truly. I feel most comfortable betting on myself. I'm not so comfortable investing in others.

What do I mean by investing in yourself? I mean using your talents or developing a new skill that will allow you to perform services for others that they'll pay for. I don't mean blowing $80,000 on an online degree only to get back into significant debt with little prospect of a big payoff.

That's not going to do you any good. It's just a huge sinkhole that will put you further behind. No, I mean using the skills you've already developed, tools that are at your disposal right now that will allow you to bank some extra cash.

Think about it for a few moments in a quiet space. Chances are you have a skill or talent of some kind that others will pay for. It may not even be a "skill," in the strict or traditional sense. It might be that you're simply willing to do some extra work that others can't or won't do.

You can profit from others' desire to not do what needs to get done. That's how you make "showing up" a skill. I'll explain that in a moment.

To Start or Not to Start...

First, let's look at what it's like to start your own business.

The statistics for starting a business are depressing. Here's some context:

- The top three challenges facing businesses, according to the National Small Business Association (NSBA), are economic uncertainty, health care and benefits, and a decline in consumer spending.
- The NSBA also says that nearly a third of existing businesses can't get funding. What's more, a study conducted by the Kauffman Firm suggests the average business needs $80,000 in capital to get started.
- *Forbes* magazine notes that 80% of businesses fail within 18 months.
- According to *Inc.* magazine, 96% of businesses fail within 10 years.

Why do most businesses fail?

I think the biggest reason is that most businesses simply don't have enough money to fund their business plan long enough for their "big idea" to catch on. So, they implode as costs eat through savings at a rapid pace.

There are other reasons as well.

For example, are you doing anything *unique*? Yes, you're a great cook, but does your city really need *another* Italian restaurant? Everyone thinks they cook the best meatballs. Their family raves about them at every holiday gathering. So, they think they can just open a restaurant for the whole city to devour those and other intergenerational delights. Bada-Bing! Strike it rich!

The reality is... not that. The reality is huge up-front costs. It's long hours. It's low profit margins. It's a hard road to a sustainable business.

Who Are You?

Peter Thiel, the remarkable entrepreneur involved with PayPal and Facebook, wrote a great book, *Zero to One*.

He talks about how competition is a destructive force. Owning a restaurant is nothing new. The lack of uniqueness, combined with high costs, almost dooms it to failure from the beginning. There might be so many Italian restaurants in your city that it's hard, if not impossible, to differentiate yourself.

Finding a unique value proposition with no competition is difficult. There's only one Google that's created market value in the hundreds of billions of dollars in the internet search engine

Invest in yourself to gain financial independence.

space, for example. This chapter isn't about trying to become a billionaire by forming a new venture.

It's about investing in you, so that you can gain financial independence.

Nor do I mean to suggest that if you are indeed a great cook that you can't capitalize on it whatsoever. An acquaintance of mine is a great cook who specializes in a specific kind of northern Thai food known as "Isan." That's the food from the region where she was born.

Rather than open a restaurant, she made three or four different dishes each day, notified her friends, and started selling out the lot by lunch. Word spread among her friends and the local ethnic community, and, soon, she had a modest but profitable business.

It fit her skillset perfectly, and she was able to exploit it without a huge cash commitment. It satisfied a need in the community because her customers wanted a taste of home and were willing to pay for it. Because the quality was high, word spread, and the business made a tidy profit.

Businesses may also fail due to a lack of focus. There's an old saying about being a jack of all trades and the master of none. Focusing on a niche can be an extremely profitable venture. Often, if you're doing something unique and the quality is high, you can get away with charging premium prices and fattening up your profit margins.

Another friend's wife has a sharp eye for vintage clothing. She specializes in dresses from the mid-20th century. Through eBay, Etsy, and other retail websites, she's been able to operate an extremely profitable business selling quality vintage dresses with a substantial mark-up. She's been successful for years.

Dresses. That's all she focuses on. She might have some competition, but she's focused and she's the *best*. She didn't expand into handbags or shoes – areas where she enjoys less of an edge and possibly suffers more competition. She stuck with what she knows, and it continues to pay off.

Do It Yourself

Most businesses fail due to cash shortfalls. So, find something that doesn't require a huge upfront cash commitment or gobs of cash to keep it running. Also, communicate your value proposition to your potential customers. Why should they hire you?

When is it time to learn a new skill? My cousin Eldo says, "If you want to learn to do something, get an estimate." What he means is, if someone tells you it's going to cost $25,000 to paint your house, you'll quickly become handy with a brush!

This is exactly what I did. I purchased a home for my elderly father to live in so he could be closer to family and reduce risk of potential injuries or accidents due to a spinal cord injury. The house needed some tender loving care to get it up to date.

The cost to paint the interior was outrageous. So, with the help of a couple family members, I tackled the project. At first, it was daunting. But, I quickly sailed up the learning curve and was painting at a level close enough to "professional" from where I stood.

Not only did I save tens of thousands of dollars. I also learned a new skill.

"Numbers guy" that I am, I ran some scenarios and figured out that by painting houses I could make $100,000 a year working 30 hours every week. There's such a shortage of labor in my dad's town; providing a quality service while undercutting the competition's outrageous prices would fill a need and still generate a hefty profit margin.

Eldo, my cousin, has become quite handy. He's redone much of his home and built beautiful gardens that produce a lot of fresh food. He's built a lovely cottage on his property as well as a huge stone deck with an outdoor grill and fire pit.

Someday, he'll be able to supplement his retirement income nicely from doing handiwork. He has a skillset that fits the context.

Doing what others don't want to do
can be quite profitable..

Take your own long look around your neighborhood. What work needs doing? What do you enjoy doing? What hobbies can you monetize? What skills can you develop?

Turn a hobby into a cash-producing enterprise. That makes it profitable and fun.

My cousin Nicky is a physical education teacher. He was a star baseball player in college. Put simply, Nicky can hit. Guess who also wants to hit a baseball? All the kids in town who play Little League and want to get better. Guess who's willing to pay good money to attend a seminar to hit a baseball? All the Joneses in the town…

It helps that Nicky has a nice personality and is well-liked. He's able to make money using a skill he developed over the years that others will happily pay for. And it costs virtually nothing to run a seminar.

Nicky also follows all the other tips and techniques in this book. He's well on his way to becoming the world's richest gym teacher.

The range of options is limitless.

I've seen folks sell organic dog treats at the local farmer's markets. These treats fly off the table – and at premium prices. Who doesn't want to give their dogs the very best and healthy treats?

I was able to paint my dad's house. But I don't have the skill or the patience to learn how to make kitchen cabinets. I also have no desire to invest in the equipment required to do a professional job. I found painting relaxing, and it didn't break the bank.

Enjoy being outdoors? Mow lawns!

I understand that this sounds like almost insultingly simple advice. But I've seen lawn quotes for $70 per mow. That's real money! It's not as much a "skill" as simply a job that other people don't want to do. There's big money to be had filling that void.

Are you a great writer? You'd be amazed how many people can use a skilled writer to produce marketing copy and professionalize their content. The key is to keep cash commitments low. Then, your side business can survive until it takes off. And, if it doesn't, you can switch gears while absorbing a small loss.

Keep that cash outflow low, and you can survive a long time. It allows you to avoid that No. 1 reason for failure: lack of capital.

If you can get your business off the ground, consider incorporating. Incorporating allows you to take advantage of tax-deferred retirement accounts, like your own 401(k), and to stash the cash at preferential rates.

Even if your business netted you $2,000 a month, you could sock away $19,000 into the 401(k). And you generate some other write-offs associated with your business that ramp up your savings ability while essentially eliminating the tax bite.

The point is, if you like to do something and you're good at it, fill a need in your local community and turn it into a profit center. Use it to your advantage. Plow that money into paying down debt and maximizing your savings.

It could catch on, and you'll be free of "The Man" all the sooner.

Chapter 5
The George Costanza School of Investing

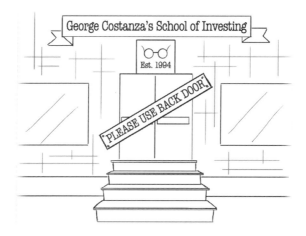

"If every instinct you have is wrong, then the opposite would have to be right." – Jerry Seinfeld

Warren Buffett is the most written-about investor in the world. No one else is even close. Millions of books have been sold claiming to reveal investing "secrets" of "The Oracle of Omaha."

There's a very good reason for that. Warren Buffett's track record is impressive. He's the wealthiest investor in the world. Someone must be No. 1. It just happens to be Warren Buffett.

Here's the rub: You're no Warren Buffett. Neither am I. I'm going to tell you the real secret. It's impossible for the average person to invest like Warren Buffett!

And there's no need to try.

Warren Buffett has huge advantages over people like you and me. Companies that want to be sold to raise some cash for long-time stakeholders will often seek Buffett out. They may offer a discounted price because he allows management to continue running the business the way they want.

With little interference, they can go about their business doing what they do best. What they do best is spit out a lot of cash flow. Buffett then gets that cash flow to reinvest in other businesses.

That's what's called a "win-win" proposition. Everyone is happy. He gets the best of both worlds: well-run businesses at a discount to true value that generate mounds of cash. And the mucky-mucks keep their jobs. Score!

Unless you can call up the CEO of Goldman Sachs at the depths of a financial crisis and loan them $5 billion at 10% interest, you don't have the same opportunities as Warren Buffett.

You can't invest like him.

A New Model

You can, however, invest like George Costanza.

George Costanza is a fictional character from "Seinfeld," one of the great sitcoms of the 1990s, if not television history. It was "a show about nothing." But there were many great insights into human nature. And it was hilarious.

Jerry Seinfeld's genius is in finding the humor in everyday life. It's really not that complicated. Take a look around, pay a little attention, and the punch line will often be right there in front of you.

Investing is the same. Take a few moments to look around, observe everyday life, and the answers are right in front of you.

Now, if you're a fan of "Seinfeld," you already know that George often gets himself in ridiculous pickles. His relationships with members of the opposite sex, his experiences in the job market, and his parents make for great humor.

George also provides an important lesson about investing.

It was near the end of season five of the long-running series. Episode No. 21 – "The Opposite" – first aired on May 21, 1994. George decides to go against his natural instincts and do the exact opposite of everything his mind tells him to do.

George, self-aware, often found himself in jams because another crazy scheme had blown up in his face. One such mess pushes him to an "a-ha!" moment: "If every instinct you have is wrong then the opposite would have to be right."

Stop for a moment. Re-read that sentence.

This one concept alone can pad your bank account by more than six times! I'll show you that math in just a moment.

George realizes that every decision he's ever made has been wrong. His life is the polar-opposite of what it should be. His luck immediately improves, however, after he orders the opposite of his usual lunch. He then spots a very pretty lady ordering the same lunch and tells her, "My name is George, I am unemployed, and I live with my parents."

To his surprise, she agrees to go out on a date with him.

Things immediately start looking up for George!

Now, consider the average investor. That's George *before* his "a-ha!" moment.

The typical investor makes the wrong decision with their money. Their investments are often the polar-opposite of what they should be.

According to DALBAR, a research company focused on measuring investor behavior, long-term data shows that investors are terrible at growing their wealth.

Over 30 years, inflation has been running at about 2.6%. But the typical equity investor has earned about 3.6%. That's despite the stock market gaining 10% annually.

Worse is that when other investments are mixed in, the return drops to just 1.6%. So, the typical investor is not even keeping up with inflation!

Now, let's look at the math. Don't worry, you only need a little multiplication here; no fancy formulas are required.

If you have $50,000 and you earn what everyone else did in stocks over 30 years, which is 3.6%, you'd have $144,465. The market return, on the other hand, made that $50,000 into $872,470.

Here's another thing you have to consider. Most people won't buy when the buying is good. Returns get dragged down by poor decisions – namely, getting scared out of stocks at market bottoms and acting too aggressively at market tops.

There are other great sources of information on individual investors.

Consider the American Association of Individual Investors. AAII's mission is to provide resources to individual investors who do their own research and manage their own portfolios. It's a noble cause.

Millions of people are members of the organization. Of course, it's not safe to assume that people actually use that education to their advantage. We know they don't. The cold-blooded part of me recognizes the edge that creates for you and me. We can exploit that lack of knowledge for our own gain.

Given AAII's large size, we can follow the actions of the group as a whole and draw some conclusions about how investors, on *average,* behave at important points along the way to financial independence.

That's not to say we need to be hyper-focused on this; the market's day-to-day gyrations are mostly random. Focusing too much attention to the 24/7 grind of global financial markets will only lead you astray.

Instead, we need to be focus on major moments. We need to be focused on extremes. Extremes don't happen every day. But they do happen often enough to provide big opportunity.

We've witnessed two key moments. The first was during the Internet Bubble of the late 1990s. Stocks would often rise 500% or more on the day they went public. In a typical week, I'd see multiple stocks with dubious underlying businesses double in value.

I was on Wall Street in 1998, right in the middle of this euphoria. I thought it was a dream… and then, of course, it turned into a nightmare.

Doctors, lawyers, and other "smart" people traded shingles to do what sounded like the right thing at the time: day-trade internet stocks.

The stock market raged higher and higher. College kids set up venture capital firms in their dorm rooms. Companies with sock puppets for mascots carried multi-billion-dollar valuations, back when a billion dollars was a billion dollars.

As I think back on those days, as we sit in the middle of what appears to be a new bubble, I have to remind myself I'm not making any of this up. I couldn't believe it then. And I can't believe it now.

During that craze, a lot of smart people did stupid things.

In March 1998, valuations had already reached stratospheric levels. Yet everyone continued to rush into stocks with everything they had… and then some. They even borrowed money to plow into stocks.

After all, where else could you double your money in just a few days? It was "dot-com logic."

Investors held the *least* amount of cash ever. According to AAII, investors held just 11% in cash compared with 74% in stocks. By the end of January 2000, right before the market was about to blow, investors held a record-setting 77% of their assets in stocks.

A lot of that money went into technology stocks. The internet was the shiny new toy.

"New rules" were invented to value these stocks. For example, Wall Street analysts used the number of "eyeballs" – or people using a website – to justify valuations.

Of course, we'd soon come to find out that cash does not flow from "eyeballs."

The craze turned into a fiasco. That bubble collapsed, and the investment portfolios of the average investor went down with it. Tech imploded, falling 78% from top to bottom. Not good.

If you take an 80% loss, you need to make 500% just to get back to even. That's no small feat. Worse yet, your mindset has likely been completely destroyed from enduring such a financial beatdown. Very few people truly recovered.

Fast-forward to 2009. The stock market had taken a beating in 2008. Lehman Brothers and Bear Stearns, two major investment banks, went belly-up. The start of 2009 was terrifying. The economy was on the brink of collapse. Or was it?

Of course, the government stepped in to back up the big banks and the major automobile companies, and the Federal Reserve slashed interest rates. Politicians and economists pulled every rabbit out of their hats to support the markets, stop the bleeding, and keep the economy alive.

It "worked," of course, and by March 2009, we now know, the stock market had bottomed. So, did the average investor load up on stocks?

No!

They did the exact opposite.

In March 2009, as the stock market was bottoming, the average investor held the *highest* level of cash ever. That cash hoard totaled 45% of their investment portfolio. Meanwhile, stocks represented just 41%.

Since then, the stock market has gone almost straight up. We've had the longest bull market in history. We've seen a few fits and starts, but overall volatility has been low, the panics short-lived.

Indeed, the Joneses probably missed the opportunity of a generation.

Know Who You Are

The best example of an investor plowing money into the markets during a crisis is Sir John Templeton.

Sir John made billions of dollars buying when others were selling and selling when others were overly optimistic about the stock market.

In 1939, he bought 100 shares of every stock trading below $1. About a third of the companies on his buy list ended up bankrupt. But the overall portfolio was worth about $40,000 just four years later! That was *a lot* of money in the early 1940s.

Templeton parlayed that into a massive, billion-dollar fortune by searching for bargains all over the world. Cha-ching!

We tend to focus on what's happening in our own backyard. If we live in the U.S., by and large our investments are in U.S. companies. That makes a certain amount of sense. And major U.S. companies also have significant overseas exposure anyway.

But, somewhere around the globe, there's probably a crisis going on. And that's where big opportunity lies.

Another great investor, the banker Baron Rothschild, said that the time to buy is when there's "blood in the streets." He followed his own advice and padded his account by backing up the truck to buy after the panic created by the Battle of Waterloo and Napoleon's defeat.

These are great tactics by masterful investors.

I, on the other hand, follow George Costanza's advice.

I like to do the exact opposite of what my best instincts tell me to do. I'm not much different from the average person. I have emotions, too. So, it's easy to get swept away by the extremes that develop as a result of markets moving this way one day, that way the next.

It's a *simple* strategy. That doesn't mean it's *easy*.

The Costanza Method just makes me stop and think about it.

Just Do This

Here's a way to make a method out of George Costanza's "madness," go against the grain, and invest only when you see "the whites of their eyes."

Watch the weekly sentiment survey from the AAII and look for times when individual investors panic over several weeks. Those moments when they begin to calm down have shown to be good "buy" signals.

So, each week, record the percentage of investors who say they're bearish. Plot a 12-week moving average.

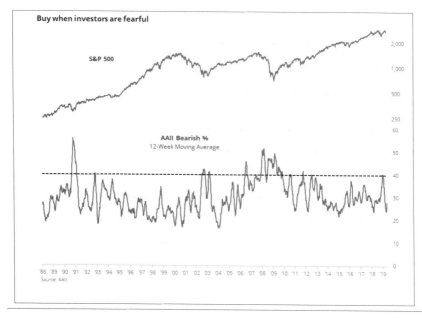

According to Sentimentrader.com, when that average climbs above 40%, that's your heads-up that people are panicking – it's almost time to buy. But that signal can flash "early" during bear markets, so conservative investors may want to wait until it drops back below 35%.

This system gave 10 "buy" signals in the past 30 years. A year later, the S&P 500 was higher all 10 times by an average of 12.7%. Over the next two years, it was 21.6% higher.

Most importantly, your downside risk over the next two years only averaged -4.1%. But your reward averaged 24.4%.

I have no problem making money in the market when others are losing it.

I like to save money when others are spending; and I like to spend money when others are saving.

In 2009, while the Global Financial Crisis was still keeping folks up at night, I needed a new car. I waited as long as I could before buying that car. I waited until there was blood in the streets.

When I walked into the dealership, there were looks of shock on the sales staff's faces. I was the only customer there that day. And I got a great deal. They didn't quite hand over the keys and let me drive the car off the lot... but it was close!

The Joneses like to blow paychecks on the latest gadgets when the world around them is rosy. It's human nature. We already know the Joneses are nothing special. It's all a façade. So, why on earth would I want to follow their lead?

Don't keep up with the Joneses. It literally pays to be a true contrarian.

When everyone is hoarding their money because their 401(k) became a 201(k) due to yet another steep selloff or "crisis," it's time to get aggressive. That's when risks are low and rewards are high.

If we're aware of what other people are doing, we can make better decisions about our own investments. The average person thinks they're "above average." We know collectively that the Joneses make poor decisions about their money.

Let's use this to our advantage.

Let's be like George Costanza.

Chapter 6

No News Is the Best News for Your Money

"The more wonderful the means of communication, the more trivial, tawdry, or depressing its contents seemed to be."
– *Arthur C. Clarke*

If you're not worried about keeping up with the Joneses, and you're paying yourself first, you're way ahead of the crowd. Consider yourself in the top 10%. Of course, that's not enough if you take that excess cash and just blow it on hair-brained investments.

That's why the George Costanza principle is so important. The more we can do the opposite of the crowd, the better off we'll be over time. While it pays to be aware of crowd behavior, we don't want our emotions to take over and to get sucked into the mass euphoria or hysteria defining the world from one day to the next.

This next step will help in that regard. It's a simple trick for getting super-wealthy.

The trick is to stop watching the news.

Tune Out

It's not an easy step to take. You'd think it would pay to be up to date on what's going on in the world. We like to feel "well informed." We like to impress our friends and colleagues at the cocktail party or the water cooler with our knowledge of current events.

But paying attention to the news is proven to be unhealthy for both your soul and your bank account.

I first realized the news was bad for my well-being in 2008 when I came home early from work because I wasn't feeling well. I lay down on the sofa and clicked on CNN's "Headline News" for some background noise.

That entire network is based on a single program running on a 30-minute loop. Still, I have lost count of how many people have been murdered, mugged, or raped; terrorist plots foiled or executed; natural disasters; and politicians doing all sorts of shady things but still not addressing in meaningful ways any of the foregoing.

It was depressing. Watching the news that day led me to think someone should launch The Good News Channel. The problem is, no one would watch it!

Good news does not sell.

I'm not alone in this feeling. In fact, there's actual research showing the news is linked to health issues. News has negative impacts on our brains.

A quick search of the internet reveals dozens of articles about how the news harms our health. The Huffington Post reports that British psychologist Dr. Graham Davey found that constant violence in the news contributes to stress, anxiety, depression, and post-traumatic stress disorder!

Another study cited by FulfillmentDaily.com showed increases in stress and negative mood after viewers watched negative news bulletins. Another 2014 study cited by the same site revealed that watching news was the largest source of stress, with nearly half of Americans citing it as a cause of their symptoms.

Now, this itself is "news." But it makes sense. A constant bombardment of negativity is bound to make us feel down.

It makes perfect sense to me that consuming the news is hazardous for your health. Here are headlines from the news section of a *New York Post* on a random day:

- 10-year-old boy starved, tortured for days before death: lawyers
- Friends, co-workers shocked by arrest of 'kindhearted' nurse charged with murdering babies
- Boss fired after telling mom her son being on life support is no reason to miss work
- Hamas used fake dating apps to gain intel on Israeli soldiers
- Why pools are facing severe lifeguard shortage
- Starbucks customer says barista mocked his disability on cup
- Dad killed sleeping wife with hammer in front of son: cops
- Fraudsters are stealing credit card information at gas stations
- Missing sex trafficked teen finally returns home: mom

I chose a random day to check out the headlines, but it's like this every day. I don't know about you, but just reading those headlines makes me depressed. My head's about to explode.

And that's before we even address the question of the accuracy of news reporting.

"Fake News"

A few times in my life, I've had first-hand knowledge of an event that was reported in the news. Literally 100% of the time, what was reported was not accurate. It's not what happened. The "news" didn't include "facts," and it was grossly misleading at best.

That experience makes me wonder about the whole enterprise.

What about the zillion events that have been reported about which I don't have any first-hand knowledge? My sample size is small, but the trend is obvious. If the news agencies are working with a perfect record of getting nothing right in the events I witnessed, how accurate is the reporting on events I know nothing about?

My best guess is that the reporting is not accurate. My solution to this problem is that I just don't pay attention.

This is even more important when it comes to your financial health.

Unfortunately, investing in financial markets has turned into a spectator sport. When I do find myself in front of financial news, I'm struck by how much the experience is like watching ESPN before the Super Bowl. But the Super Bowl happens just one Sunday in February. The stock market is open almost every weekday of the year.

That's a problem if your goal is to build long-term wealth.

Later in the book, I share strategies that rely on no news information to build wealth. One is "The 30-Second Millionaire." If you follow that strategy – and it takes just a few seconds here and there – you'll likely be in the top 1% of all investors over time... yep, an honest-to-goodness one-percenter.

You won't get there by watching "experts" talk over each other, waving their hands in the air just like the former NFL players do to prime the pregame crowd.

Most of them wear fancy suits, sport perfectly coiffed hair, and seem to know what they're talking about. But it's all theatrics. There's even a guy with Bozo the Clown hair who rips heads off stuffed animals. It's a carnival show.

That's CNBC I'm talking about there, not ESPN, just to be perfectly clear.

I don't really see anything entertaining about the process of building wealth. It's not a game show. It's not a sporting event. It's not reality TV. It's serious business. It's your hard-earned money working for you to provide a better life over time.

What I'm about to tell you is bad for my own career. I've been a guest on CNBC and Fox Business Channel. I've been profiled in *Barron's* and *Investor's Business Daily*. And I've been featured in a full-color spread in the *Wall Street Journal*.

But here it is, in simple terms: The financial news is hazardous to your wealth. Avoid it as much as you can.

Build a Long-Term Filter

To achieve unbounded wealth, we need to think and focus on the long term. That's the only kind of foundation to consistently apply our method to achieve the results we desire.

Following along with the moment-to-moment, day-to-day, even week-to-week and month-to-month fluctuations of the stock market/casino is not necessary. And those moves need not impact our thinking. The news is designed to get us to act at precisely the wrong time and do the exact opposite of what we should do.

Almost all the noise in the stock market is random. Stocks move 20% on nothing more than the normal ebbs and flows of nature. The problem is, we feel the need to be able to explain those ebbs and flows. We're human, and we want to know "why."

One day the stock market is down, and the "experts" have an explanation for it. The very next day, that explanation is refuted, and the stock market goes up. Complex theories make the person explaining them seem smart. Then, we seem smart when we tell our neighbors or our friends all the complicated reasons why the financial markets are doing this or that.

You and I could sit around developing theories for why birds fly south for the winter or we could just accept that it happens.

Sometimes, the stock market goes up or down simply because it wants to go up or down. No explanation is needed. It just happens.

The need to understand "why" and answer those questions makes us feel smarter than the next person. In reality, no one knows why most of this stuff is fluctuating around.

For every person that comes up with reasons that justifies why the stock market is going to go up, there's another person with a perfectly good reason for why it should go down. After all, for every buyer there needs to be a seller. When there isn't a match, prices move – up and/or down – until there is.

Truthfully, no one really knows. Only liars call stock market tops and bottoms perfectly.

"More buyers than sellers" or "more sellers than buyers" are the only explanations. There's your line to drop at the cocktail party or the water cooler.

The bottom line is news gets in the way of our goals.

If you get bogged down by the analysis of every oscillation in your portfolio, every reason why the market is up or down, every explanation for monetary policy at a given point in time, it's nothing but interference.

Let's take some examples from recent history.

One of the few times I watched TV in recent years was the night of November 8, 2016. I tuned in to follow reporting of returns for the 2016 presidential election. Talk about a spectator sporting event! I felt like I should've been nibbling from a bucket of popcorn while I switched between CNN and Fox News throughout the night.

I had a keen interest in the election because I knew whoever won, history would be made. Early on, Hillary Clinton jumped out to a lead. Over the course of the night, which dragged into the next day, Donald Trump gained steam. Then, he took the lead. Then, he won.

And that's when it got interesting. I looked at the overnight futures market and noticed that it was tanking. Stocks were taking an absolute beating. Initially, the markets didn't want Donald Trump, a businessman, as president. Why? Who knows. My guess is that with Hillary Clinton, market participants were confident they knew what they were getting. She's "status quo," and markets don't like surprises.

That's a guess. I don't know. I do know that making guesses is a quick way to do the wrong thing at the wrong time.

To wit, from November 8 to November 9, the market reversed course and rebounded quickly. It turned on a dime and soared.

Now, the 2016 election was perhaps the most emotional shared experience of that year. Election Day was a few weeks before Thanksgiving. Many friends, families, and loved ones across the United States were pitted against each other at the dining room table. It was raw for a long while. It still is.

I was in Washington, D.C., a month after the election. I had dinner with a group of people, one of whom worked on the Democratic campaign. He had hoped to work in digital media for the White House after the election. That was his dream job. When Hillary Clinton lost the election, that shattered his dream.

Reading about the markets' daily squiggles gets in the way of building wealth.

I don't think I've ever seen someone so depressed by the outcome of an election. By the end of the dinner, I was quite worried about his mental and physical health.

This is an important lesson: There is no room for emotion in financial markets.

My dinner companion's behavior suggests there's no room for emotion in any business – markets, politics, or otherwise.

It's totally understandable to be upset if your candidate didn't win an election. But don't let it affect your path to unbounded wealth. It's important to keep moving forward toward your goals. Had you been emotional about the 2016 election results, it could've moved you off your path in a big way.

That emotion is probably reflected in the tremendous volatility in the markets as the election results unfolded. Over time, it won't make a lick of difference to your path to financial freedom.

Consider the beating global markets took when Great Britain voted to leave the European Union after over 40 years as a key member of the economic bloc. If you watched the financial news, the "Brexit" vote was a complete disaster. It was time to bail out of stocks. The world was coming to an end!

But, then, a remarkable thing happened. The stock market quickly recovered and reached new highs over the next several weeks. The stock market totally shrugged off this *major* economic event.

If you reacted to the vote by selling off part of your portfolio, it may have cost you tens of thousands of dollars, or more.

"It Just Doesn't Matter"

Here's another quick tip: If you don't know the level of the Dow Jones Industrial Average, you're probably way ahead of your market-savvy neighbor.

The day to day reading of an equity index – no matter how big – is not relevant to building long-term wealth. When I talk about the market with friends, neighbors, and new acquaintances as well, I often like to lead with a bit of a thought experiment.

I'll choose a random date, and I'll ask, "What happened to the stock market on March 7, 2008?" After I get a blank stare for a few moments, I'll answer my own question by saying, "I have absolutely no idea what happened to the stock market on that day."

It just doesn't matter.

In 30 years, it'll be completely pointless to know what level the stock market indexes are trading at today. March 7, 2008, became irrelevant much sooner than that!

If you're clueless about the day to day ups and downs of the markets and the economy, let's keep it that way. Ditch the news. It's counterproductive.

Since we already know that most people do the wrong thing at the wrong time, we must be mentally fit in order to plod along our course to financial freedom.

Don't let the news drag you down and get you depressed. Turn off the TV, step away from the computer, set down your handheld, get some fresh air, and clear you head!

Chapter 7
Double Your Retirement in 5 Minutes

"There are some men whose only mission among others is to act as intermediaries; one crosses them like bridges and keeps going."
– Gustave Flaubert

Many financial advisors charge high fees for their advice. They live large. What about their clients?

It's one of those stories that still circulates on Wall Street, the basics of which sometimes pop up as the basis for an ad for a discount brokerage or two. It's about a 1920s-era gentleman walking along the waterfront admiring all the fancy yachts. Informed the big boats belong to freshly minted financial hotshots, our gentleman, looking confused, wonders, "Where are all the customers' yachts?"

That's a good question!

Death, Taxes, and Fees

Only two of those things are certain.

If you have a financial advisor, chances are you're overpaying. That's for a lot of extraneous advice as well as for investment products. They get rich selling you overpriced wares. At the same time, high fees eat into your savings and your returns – dramatically. I like to say that the easiest way to double your retirement in just a few minutes is to fire your financial advisor, or switch to lower fee investment products.

Let's say you're paying 2% to have your wealth managed. You've done well, socking away $200,000 with 30 years to go until retirement. If you make 7% annually, which is a very respectable return, paying that 2% annualized fee results in $658,000 *less* over those 30 years than if you paid nothing at all.

That's the power of compounding – in a negative way.

Free advice is rarely free.

On the other hand, if you pay 1% instead of 2%, you have $284,000 more fattening your wallet over 30 years.

That's a big difference. It's likely that $284,000 can fund *years* of retirement living.

Look, you're going to pay some sort of fee for just about every service you engage. There's always a cost embedded somewhere. Not much is free in this world, most certainly not financial advice.

Many types of accounts generate high but hard-to-find fees.

One is a "wrap account." Under this arrangement, the custodian of your money charges a fee based on all of your assets under management. Think of it as a fee that "wraps" everything all into one. This fee covers administrative, research, and other costs. One advantage of paying a flat fee or percentage of your assets is that your account can't be churned. "Churning" is when your broker buys and sells a lot of investment products to generate commissions and fatten his paycheck. Meanwhile, your pocket is being picked.

Even if you don't trade much, a wrap account can help the brokerage company suck more and more money out of your account.

Consider the case of Josephine DesParte, who at 88 had $8 million invested in some bonds, cash, and just three stocks. One stock was that of her former employer, and the other two were spun off from that company. In all, they paid her over $100,000 in annual dividends. Not bad!

There's not a lot of action in that account. I can tell you, it wasn't all that profitable for the brokerage firm. So, they moved her into a wrap account and diversified her investments. That led to $120,000 in annual fees and $320,000 in capital gains taxes on Ms. Josephine's account.

She sued the brokerage for wrongful investments and losses and won a $1.1 million settlement.

Unload

Mutual fund "loads" present another potential trap.

A mutual fund is a professionally managed vehicle with assets pooled by a bunch of people to invest in stocks, bonds, or other asset classes. A "load" is a commission a broker earns by investing your money into a mutual fund.

Loads can be high, like 5% of the assets invested. That's a pretty big hurdle for you to overcome right from the very get-go, and it dramatically impacts the long-term performance of your investments.

Loads are a load of crap. Investors should unload their loaded funds and find better options elsewhere.

The same goes for "redemption" fees. A redemption fee is what you pay if you sell a fund before your money has been invested for a certain length of time.

In general, I agree with the concept that you should not be overtrading your account and moving it around from fund to fund. We've discussed the fact that most investors buy and sell at the wrong time. A redemption fee makes this game of musical fund chairs more expensive.

But it is your money, after all, and if you want to sell out of a fund, you should be able to.

Know What You Own

In addition to reviewing your statements and discussing with your advisor the fees you're paying, you need to analyze what you actually own!

First, a broker may be better incentivized to place you in certain types of investments. For example, an annuity can carry a commission of as much as 10%. That's outrageous!

Consider the Oppenheimer Rochester Maryland Municipal Bond Fund. That's a long name, a little challenging to say in one

Don't let Wall Street fat cats get rich off your hard work.

breath. But it basically looks like the fund should hold municipal bonds in Maryland. Or is it Rochester?

Municipal bonds are debt issued by a state or local government to finance projects like roads and bridges.

In January of 2017, just 52.1% of the bonds held by this fund were from Maryland issuers. A whopping 35% of the bonds it held were from Puerto Rico.

The problem with that is that Puerto Rico has tens of billions of dollars of debt, and little way to repay it or even service it. The Caribbean island is in full crisis mode.

Given the name of the fund, you'd be justified thinking you own a lot of Maryland municipal bonds. But the manager has looked elsewhere in a quest for higher yields. In effect, this creates huge risks in a relatively "safe" investment class.

The managers didn't do anything they're not allowed to do. But it may come as a surprise that a Maryland bond fund owns roughly only half its investments in, well, Maryland!

If you add in sales charges, the fund has made 2.24% annually since inception as of mid-February 2017.

The moral of the story is simple: Know what you own! It just goes to show that it's never safe to assume that it's safe to assume!

Down With Fees

The good news is that fees are coming down. Also, there are more cost-effective ways to manage money than there were even 10 years ago.

It's funny the way the market responds to informed demand in a free economy.

ETFs, trade on public markets and are bought and sold just like stock in a company such as IBM. They were introduced in the early 1990s, but they've gathered tremendous momentum in just the past five years.

Because you can trade them like stocks, you can avoid loads and redemption fees. Overall, fees have fallen sharply; in some cases, ETFs can be traded commission-free. On average, you can purchase an ETF on the total stock market for about 0.03%.

The broad movement is in the direction of zero-fee funds. Of course, sometimes you get what you pay for. It could be too much of a good thing. And some of the "zero-fee" funds I've seen do not guarantee that there will not be fees levied at a later date. Buyer beware.

Specialty ETFs will often have higher fees. And there may be valid reasons to hold such funds in your portfolio.

For example, you may want to provide some downside protection to your portfolio. You can do this with a "hedge." You can create a downside hedge by betting against stocks that are expected to decline due to fundamental pressures such as increased competition or aggressive accounting.

Or, the hedge may be in asset classes harder for an individual to trade, like high-yield bonds. You're going to pay more here. It requires a specialized skill to manage these types of investments.

Other ETFs that may carry higher fees are sector- or country-related vehicles. For example, you can invest in the technology sector. You can narrow that down and invest in just semiconductors or cybersecurity stocks. If you want to explore the globe, you can purchase ETFs focused on Russia or China.

We can justify the use of specialty ETFs and the higher fees they charge because they help us accomplish specific, discrete goals.

Overall, though, we're significantly limiting return loss due to fees and commissions because the core of our investment strategy is holding the total stock market or the total bond market.

We're not here to churn through high-priced products with little to no discernible value.

ETFs are fully transparent. That means you know exactly what they own.

Every day, holdings of a particular vehicle will be listed on the sponsoring firm's website for the entire world to see.

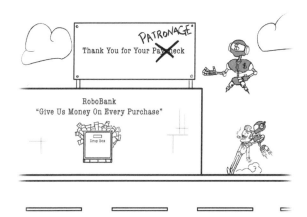

Beware the hidden costs of banking advisors.

So, there are no excuses about being blindsided if the ETF owns some bonds in a far-flung place in full crisis mode.

The Mobile Future

Everything is going digital. And one of the hottest sectors in finance is so-called robo-advisors.

These are sophisticated models that take your age, income, savings rate, expenses, and other factors and create an investment portfolio on your behalf. But these platforms can be flawed in big ways.

For example, the model may force you to hold more cash than is needed at your current age and income level. Over a long period of time, cash can act as a drag on your investment performance, especially in the world of ultra-low interest rates we live in today.

There's a hidden cost, too. The robo-advisor is making money off that cash, while you get nothing for parking it in a short-term money market account.

These robo-advisors also invest in index funds. That makes sense, given that the model needs historical data to draw conclusions about what asset classes to be invested in. An active manager who picks stocks to own and isn't pegged to an index can have performance results that are all over the map. That manager could be very hot for 10 years only to flame out entirely in the next bear market.

But, with an index, you pretty much know what you're getting.

There are two basic types of indexes. The first is an index where the stocks are weighted by their market capitalization. So, bigger companies get a bigger weight. If Apple represents 5% of the total market value of all the companies in the index, it will get assigned 5% of the weight in the index.

Meanwhile, the tiniest company may be worth a fraction of Apple. Call it 0.01%. So, it'll get assigned that weight and have almost no impact on the performance of the index.

The second type of index is captured in the term "smart beta." There's really nothing particularly "smart" about them. They just weight the stocks in the index differently. The smart beta portfolio may weight companies by sales, earnings, dividends, cash flow, earnings quality, or any combination of factors.

Let's say the smart beta portfolio uses earnings growth to weight the stocks. Under this scenario, Apple might only be 2% of the overall weight. Meanwhile, our little company has huge earnings growth. So, while its market value is tiny, it would be weighted much higher in the smart beta portfolio.

Index funds make allocating money to different sectors and asset classes relatively easy. But easy is not always better.

One of the larger problems I see with robo-advisors is that these are static portfolios. They don't shift based on market trends, valuation, or sentiment. And they don't hedge. They also became very popular *after* the last bear market. So, they're relatively untested in the real world; it's still too early to tell whether clients can stick with it through thick and thin. Studies about investor behavior show that we should have our doubts.

By not hedging, these portfolios make more money on the way up. But they almost certainly lose a lot more on the way down. So, they don't account for the ride you're going to take along the way to your retirement goals. This is the "investment rollercoaster" we discuss in Chapter 9.

If you lose 10% on your money, it only takes 11% to get back to even. But if you lose 50% on an investment, it takes a 100% return to get back to square one! So, it's well worth it to avoid huge losses. It could take decades to make them up.

We live in a world where everyone has their head buried in their smartphone. Just because there's a website or an app for it doesn't make it the best way to go about things.

Your retirement and financial goals are very important to you! It's a highly individualized process. Don't mindlessly follow the robo-advisor crowd.

It's Your Money

Maybe you don't want to fire your financial advisor. Maybe he does have your best interest in mind. Nevertheless, it's something to review in terms of what you're invested in and what the costs are.

Not all advisors are bad. Some do great work. You may need an advisor simply to enforce discipline to follow an investment strategy. Paying for that can be worth its weight in gold. But make sure you know that your interests come first. I'll hammer home again and again that the most important thing you can do is *stick with your process*.

For some people, a computer model offering a menu of investment options will do the trick. For others, hiring a financial advisor and meeting with them periodically will work wonders.

Finally, many people will simply be best doing this on their own.

And that's okay too.

Because it's your money. Here's to turning it into real wealth!

Chapter 8
Every Stock Has a Middle Name: Danger

"By failing to prepare, you are preparing to fail."
– Benjamin Franklin

A lot of money's been made by people giving advice to buy stocks and hold them for the long term. "Long-term buy-and-hold" is what they say the average investor ought to be doing. An entire niche has been built around "stocks for the long run." Over time, they argue, there's no better place to put your money than the stock market. For the type of time horizon you're talking about, the returns are always huge.

Of course mutual funds want you to buy funds and hold them for the long term because that's how they make money, by charging you fees for investing your money!

When people tell me about outsized returns they're making, I like to tell them the story of Jesus. Yes, *that* Jesus. But it's not a story from the Bible. Rather, it's a story about compounding wealth.

Let's just say for the sake of argument that you roamed the earth around the time of Jesus and had a whopping net worth of $0.01. You have a single shiny penny in your pocket. It doesn't seem like much, does it? But, if that $0.01 compounded at 3% (just three percent…) annually, today your heirs would have…

$458,788,143,260,473,000,000,000.00.

I don't know how much money that is. I can't count that high, nor can I really wrap my head around that number. I know it's a lot! It might even be all the money in the world!

So, the notion that stocks are going to earn 10% over the long run rings a bit false to me. I think it's a very dangerous assumption. Your returns depend on a lot of factors.

Day One

First, your returns depend greatly on when you start investing.

If you started investing in October 1929, right before Black Thursday, your returns would be weighed down for decades to get back to even. That's going to be a tough row to hoe mentally. The same thing happened from the late 1960s through the early 1980s.

We don't know what the future holds. That the market rebounded fairly quickly after the last crash in 2008 is no indication how it will recover from the next one.

And there will be a next one. We just don't know when.

Second, investing in individual stocks is very dangerous. The road to investment success is paved with landmines. I co-authored a book on financial crookery called *What's Behind the Numbers?*

The research that informed that book also tells me one of the dangers of investing in individual stocks is that those companies are managed by human begins. Humans are motivated by fear and greed. We always have been, and we always will be.

That greed is really on display when it comes to corporate management teams. They have huge incentives to keep a stock price flying high. Why? Well, they often have massive stock-option grants and salaries to protect.

They need to keep the stock price up. Their jobs depend on it. Their own finances depend on it.

So, when business hits a bump in the road on the way to their personal prosperity, there's a temptation to cheat here and there.

There are numerous ways management teams can act aggressively to put their own interests ahead of yours, to pull the wool over investors' eyes by making the financial performance look better than it truly is.

In a nutshell, there are plenty of *legal* ways to cheat. Sad, but true.

Here's an example that happens all the time. Management could offer an incentive to a customer to sign a contract today that would otherwise have been signed at a later date.

What are the incentives to do so? Well, management could lower the price, offer longer payment terms, or even throw in Super Bowl tickets. This allows management to record the revenue today rather than a quarter or two down the road.

So, all things being equal, the current quarter's revenue is overstated. Management stole it from the future. This is called "stuffing the channel."

Management could also treat an expense as an asset. This would lower expenses and prop up earnings. This is all legal. And it distorts the true earnings power of the company.

Why is this important? Well, let's say a company earns $1, and Wall Street analysts forecast it'll earn $1.20 next year. Year-over-year earnings growth of 20% sounds great!

But if $0.20 of that dollar came from bogus shenanigans, the company really only earned $0.80 on a sustainable basis. So, now, they have to grow 50% (from $0.80 to $1.20) instead of 20%. And if they're really aggressive this year, there will be fewer rabbits to pull out of their hats to make that $1.20 estimate for next year.

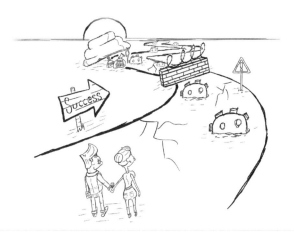

The road to success is filled with land mines.

When Wall Street's disappointed, stock prices tank. And you get caught holding the bag.

All this trickery happened right under your nose. But, if you're not looking at the right things, you'll never see it coming. This can go on for a long time.

Eventually, though, executives get caught with their hands in the cookie jar and bad behavior catches up with them.

Unless you're prepared to dig into the abyss that is the Securities and Exchange Commission database of financial and operating statements and results from publicly traded companies, it's best to avoid individual stock-picking.

Simple Numeracy Will Do

You don't have to be a propeller-head accountant to understand what's behind the numbers. You don't need an advanced financial degree to catch management teams with their hands in the cookie jar. But it is a lot of hard work.

Unbounded wealth is about simplifying things. So, take a deep breath. Relax. You don't have to read annual and quarterly earnings reports, proxy statements, and prospectuses.

You do need to have a basic foundation for understanding why certain investments may not be worth the risk. Apart from the fact that most firms use accounting to pretty-up their financial results, investing in stocks is dangerous for another reason.

That reason is capitalism.

You see, with capitalism, there are a lot of losers and very few winners.

We all know this through real world experience. For some reason, when we think about the stock market, we often forget – or overlook – this risk. We're blinded by glossy stories about companies changing the world and the huge gains we stand to reap thereby.

Walmart moves into town, and all the small regional retailers go out of business. Home Depot sets up shop, and the local hardware store goes the way of the dodo.

Microsoft grew to dominate the PC software business while its competitors died off one by one. Forty years ago, there were numerous spreadsheet and word-processing programs on the market. Now, there's pretty much one, Mr. Softy.

When I started my career on Wall Street in the late 1990s, there were a lot of companies in the online search business. Many of them had huge market values. Yahoo! was the clear leader. Later on, along came Google. Yahoo! fell by the wayside, never really recovered, and is now buried inside Verizon Communications.

Google became so powerful that it's become a verb. You don't search for something on the internet anymore; you "Google" it. If it's not a rule it should be: First in the dictionary makes you the leader!

Someday, though, something new will replace Google.

Who knows?

Let's Get Real

When it comes to investing in stocks, the average person thinks, "The stock market goes up over time, so I'll buy some stocks, hold them for the long term, and I'll be rich."

Unh-unh. Nope. It doesn't work that way.

If we were talking in 1979 and I told you that in 30 years Eastman Kodak, General Motors, Bethlehem Steel, General Electric, and Polaroid would all be either bankrupt or on life-support, you'd call me crazy, at the very least.

Once upon a time, those were the stocks to own. You couldn't go wrong with them. Indeed, they were the lynchpins of what was called the "Nifty Fifty." Just buy those stocks, sit out by your backyard pool sunning yourself and drinking Martinis… life was grand.

But strange things happened, and capitalism got in the way. New technologies emerged. Tastes changed. Other countries pulled themselves up by their bootstraps and became more competitive, places like Japan and Korea and China and Vietnam.

The winners of the past rarely endure long into the future. Who knows what'll happen to Apple, Facebook, Google, and Tesla?

One of my favorite stock market studies is called *The Capitalism Distribution*. It was conducted by a firm called BlackStar Funds. It's a revealing look into what drives stock market returns.

From 1983 through 2006, the stock market, as measured by the Russell 3000 Index, was mostly in bull market mode! The good times were a rollin'. Making money in the stock market was a piece of cake! Just throw a dart at the stock pages, and you'd nail a winner. Everyone was getting rich!

Or were they?

While the market was roaring, 39% of stocks lost money. Yeah, *losers*. Here is some more data from *The Capitalism Distribution*:

- 18.5% of stocks lost 75% or more! Ouch.
- 64% of stocks underperformed the Russell 3000 Index. Not good.
- The average stock returned about 0%. No gain, lots of pain.
- Only about 25% of stocks accounted for the overall market's gains. Good luck!

When looking at the stock market through a winners-and-losers frame, it really looks like one big casino.

Unfortunately, individual investors are the patsies.

The odds of selecting a huge winner are about 16 to one.

Of course, you also have to hold that stock for decades, through thick and thin, including multiple 50% declines. You might have better luck renting a tuxedo, heading to Vegas, ordering a Vesper, and dropping $10,000 on "00" and "7" on the roulette table.

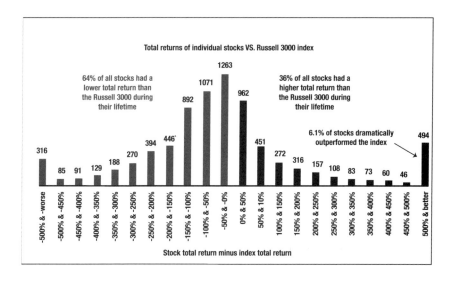

When we begin to build portfolios, we'll discuss "asset classes." An asset class is a whole group of securities – like stock indexes, bonds, and commodities. This type of investing eliminates much of the risk of buying individual companies.

However, some of you will get the itch to dabble in a few shares here and there. I can hear it already: "But, John, I want to buy some stocks!"

Later, we'll turn our attention to a simple strategy based on individual stocks. Armed with sound technique and backed by research, it gives us a standing chance of beating the odds and juicing our returns.

It's important to understand, early on in your process of establishing financial independence, that the only way to venture into individual stocks is with a proper set of tools. Not only that, you must know how to use these tools.

The goal is to separate companies that put their interests ahead of yours as a shareholder from those that pay you first. The ability to do that comes from understanding the quality of the company's financial reporting.

This is *your* money. This isn't a court of law. Every company is guilty until proven innocent.

If you really want to own stocks, start with that mindset and work backward; that's how to find the highest-quality opportunities.

What won't we do, ever? We won't chase "hot tips."

"Hot tips" are recipes for disaster. I can't tell you how many times I'm asked about a particular stock someone's been "hot tipped" on. Neither they nor the "hot tipper" has done any personal, original research.

They're all suspect... a guy heard a guy talking about a stock in the locker room of the local YMCA. Suddenly, it's the Next Big Thing.

If you have excess cash and you want to use a portion of it to grow your net worth, or if you have a genuine interest in stocks, it's important to establish a well-defined strategy.

"Hot tips" don't help. Neither does acting on impulse. It's best to approach the market of stocks with cold blood. Flying by the seat of your pants, fired by emotion, will get you nowhere.

Buckle up. Investing in stocks will be a wild run. But, as you'll see, it's fun, too!

Chapter 9

The World's Scariest Rollercoaster – No Ticket Required!

"Markets can remain irrational a lot longer than you and I can remain solvent." – John Maynard Keynes

Life is full of ups and downs. Of course, you've experienced times in your life when everything went right. You felt good. You slept well. Work was easy. You even enjoyed the commute! Your relationships were solid. The kids were smiling. Everything was grand.

It continued that way, until it didn't. Then there were some downs. Maybe you didn't feel well. Work wasn't so grand. Gridlock started to grind on you. It was always "too loud" at home, and the kids were grumpy.

Maybe those downs continued for a while. When it rains, it pours!

Financial markets are the same way. There are ups, and there are downs. Lots of them. Markets can move one way or the other in big, violent reversals. Those moves may not even make sense from a practical standpoint.

For example, individual stocks can move up or down 30% on no news at all. That seems strange. How can hundreds of billions of dollars in value be gained or lost with no news? Beats me; happens all the time.

There's even a fancy word for it: "volatility."

Be More Smooth

"Volatility" just means that stuff moves up and stuff moves down. If you read enough books "about Wall Street" (you only *need* this one…), you'll often find that volatility is considered a bad thing.

The experts think that if things move around too much, that's bad. The experts create all sorts of complex formulas to "reduce" exposure to volatility. It never works in the real world, and the mathematicians lose billions of dollars of other people's money.

This happens every economic cycle. The failure of complex failures eventually led to the Global Financial Crisis and the Great Recession.

The Holy Grail for these knuckleheads is what are called "low volatility" vehicles. Here's a pro tip: That's a loser's strategy.

"Volatility" isn't necessarily a bad thing. It is simply how much a stock's or a bond's or a commodity's price moved up or moved down. The more movement it makes, the more volatile it is.

Here's the thing, though: A lot of movement might not be bad. In fact, it can be *good*. Indeed, "absolutes" are for suckers.

Consider for a moment a stock you buy. Let's call it Four-Bagger Inc., trading on the New York Stock Exchange under the ticker symbol HMRN.

You buy HMRN on Monday for $5 per share. On Wednesday, Four-Bagger gets bought out by Fastball Corp. at $10 a share! You make a 100% return in two days. That's a great bet. You're lucky, too!

But that's *very* volatile.

A 100% move in a couple days is rare. However, all the volatility was to the upside. Your investment went straight up. Who cares what the experts think about the volatility? You should pat yourself on the back. You made a nice score, a home run…

Let's look at another situation. You buy a stock on Monday for $5, Twin Killing Ltd., trading on the Nasdaq Stock Market under the ticker symbol OUT.

On Wednesday, OUT goes down to $2.50 because management announced some bad news. Maybe a major customer canceled an order, or a factory exploded because of a gas leak. Right, Twin Killing is down and out.

But, six months later, business recovers and OUT gets bought for $10 a share. That's also very volatile.

OUT didn't go straight up. That first 50% decline was death-defying. At that point, most normal investors would've bailed on the investment. Yet, eventually, everything righted itself. And in the end the return it gave was significant, in a short period of time.

That's volatility.

Volatility is not our enemy. We are our own worst enemy.

You. You! YOU!

Let me explain what I mean when I say we're our own worst enemy.

We've talked about how to generate some cash to invest for your future. Before we get to specifics about portfolios and how we can invest to grow our pile of Benjamins, we have to tackle one last hurdle.

And it's a big one: the psychology of investing.

This is a big topic on Wall Street today. A lot of boring books and boring articles have been written on what the eggheads, the head-shrinkers, and the term-droppers call "behavioral finance." It's a hot topic of debate in academia, among clinicians, and among Wall Street's well-known collection of deviant profiles.

I'm not a professor. I don't even own a tweed jacket with suede elbow patches, nor do I smoke a pipe.

There's no need to lie down on a sofa and have your head examined by some high-priced therapist, though. Nor will I bore you with more fancy terms and fresh case studies. That sort of stuff might make me seem intelligent. But it's not going to get you to do anything to identify and achieve your goals.

I don't want to put you to sleep. I want to activate you.

You: That's all that matters.

So, here's a practical approach to "behavioral finance." I've broken it down to concepts you'll be able to digest and use. So, it's very simple.

There are five key steps to successful investing:

- Identify a strategy that fits your personality and;
- Stick with it;
- Stick with it through thick;
- Stick with it through thin;
- Stick with it through hell and high water.

These steps are simple. They are not *easy*. But stick with it.

Picture a Rollercoaster

No investment portfolio develops in a straight line. Nothing does. If that were the case, we could just buy literally any stock or any bond, plant ourselves on the beach, order a few Bahama Mamas, periodically surf on over via our handheld computer of choice, click on our account summary page, and watch the pie grow...

Life like that would be boring.

No, my friend, there are going to be ups, and there are going to be downs. And those downs – and even those ups, in different ways, of course – will be scary. Hopefully, you'll get to experience what it's like to have a fat portfolio at what looks like a market top.

That's why we have to get control of our emotions. That's why we have to understand ourselves and how we'll react to that rollercoaster ride. The type of investments you make, of course, will determine how severe those ups and downs are.

If you own only stocks, you're going to experience several 30% to 50% drops in your lifetime. It's just the way it is. Anyone who says anything different doesn't know what they're talking about or isn't telling you the truth.

Own the stock market long enough, you're going to suffer several 30% to 50% declines, maybe worse on a percentage basis, maybe more than several. Get your mind and your heart and your stomach ready for the ride you're going to take.

You'll also likely end up with the most money. That's the payoff over long periods of time for sitting through a lot of volatility.

Some people can deal with that sort of stomach-churning volatility. Most people can't. And that's okay. It's not about who has thicker skin, or whose nerves most closely resemble steel.

The aim is to position you to achieve your goals, to set you on a course that lets you live on your own terms.

What matters most is what you – no one else – can stomach. I can give you some tools to better your finances. I can give you some encouraging words along the way. I can't trade the stocks for you. I can't make you hang in there when you've lost half of your investment portfolio – poof! – like that.

Only you can focus on you and only you.

That's how you get out of whatever rut it is that made you get this far in this book. That's how we avoid falling back into the trap of trying to keep up with the Joneses. That's how you recover when you've lost half your investment portfolio.

The most important decision you make is choosing a strategy that fits your personality so that you stick with it.

Human beings forgetting they're human beings is what makes them vastly underperform the market. It's as simple as that. Data from the American Association of Individual Investors confirm, despite all their researching and all their educating, most people buy and sell at exactly the wrong time.

One of my favorite case studies is that of Ken Heebner. Heebner's managed a ton of money; he's been well-known in investing circles for decades. He's been highly praised, too. He makes big bets, and when they pay off, they pay off huge.

By the end of the first decade of the 21st century, he'd racked up the best returns of any diversified stock fund manager. He was No. 1. Someone has to be No. 1, and it happened to be Heebner.

He generated a whopping 18% annually, which was well ahead of his competitors. If an investor placed money with Heebner and just left it there, they'd most likely be well ahead of the Joneses. And, that's exactly what most of those investors got, right?

Not exactly…

Despite 18% annualized gains for Heebner's fund, the average investor *lost* 11% annually over the same period!

Say what…

Yep, that's what happened. The average investor in the *best* manager's fund of the decade got completely spanked and lost a bundle.

Yep, these investors were either lucky enough or had the insight to invest in the best money manager available to them.

Numero Uno… The Big Kahuna… Ken Heebner…

Those return numbers, of course, are based on cash coming into and out of the fund.

In a nutshell, investors bought into the fund after Heebner's scorching-hot streak with his stock picks; he'd already racked up big gains. And they bailed on him after he went cold. They fouled the whole thing up by chasing returns. And they ended up with nothing.

Ungatz!

Investing in stocks can lead to the most money, but the ride is death-defying.

Had they stashed cash in the fund after every cold streak, the returns would've been higher than 18% annualized. That's the best time to invest with a truly skilled manager. It's not when he's winning. It's when he's on a cold streak. That way, if performance returns to normal, you should get a big boost as prices "revert to the mean."

In our book *Rule of 72*, my co-author Tom Jacobs and I called this "Getting the Heebner Jeebies." That's far more enlightening than some technical term about human behavior and investing activity.

Most people simply get the Heebner Jeebies by buying and selling at exactly the wrong time.

We can avoid serious cases of the Heebner Jeebies by *religiously* following a strategy that fits our personality.

We have to align ourselves for returns that don't give us nausea.

But the ride will be wild.

What's Your Ticket?

Think about investing like you do the experience at an amusement park.

There are all sorts of people at these places. A couple years ago, I visited Walt Disney's place in Orlando for the first time in 35 years. My friend was getting married. I had a free day before the wedding, so I spent it at Epcot Center.

On one ride, you sit in a capsule and get shot up to "Mars". Along the winding way to the attraction itself, there are a bunch of signs warning you to turn back if you have a heart condition or are afraid of heights.

I'm sure the lawyers insisted on the placement of these signs. They'll ruin the fun for everyone, even in Disney's world.

When I did get to the line, there was a married couple in front of me. As we got to the front and the man squeezed into the capsule, he said, "What the f**k!" Yep, it was pretty tight in there… and a bit scary.

Finally, we blasted off. My heart was in my stomach. In the end, it was fun. There were also a few moments of rattled nerves.

If the death defying all-stocks ride scares you, choose something a bit less nerve-wracking.

That's what it is when you get involved with financial markets and investing: thrills, spills, chills… you get it all.

If you don't mind being strapped in by the neck, waist, knees, and ankles, owning a portfolio heavily weighted to stocks might be right for you. As we've talked about, over long periods of time, you'll probably end up with the most money.

On the other hand, if you can't stick with the strategy, it's pointless. Books have been written about owning stocks for 200 years or more and how the returns top every other investment opportunity. I don't know about you, but I don't plan to live 200 years. I don't even want to think what a 200-year-old me might even look like!

So, looking out over 200 years doesn't work for me. We have to think relative to where and when we are.

Remember, investors held the most amounts of cash in modern history at the market bottom in 2009. That's precisely the time to buy stocks. That's when it was scariest. That ended up being the most rewarding.

Most people never saw the benefit.

If you can see those 30% to 50% dips as opportunities to load up on more stock – in other words, if you can do the opposite of what everyone else is doing – then, by George Costanza, more stocks and less of everything else should work for you.

Somewhere in the middle reduces the death-defying G-forces. You're still probably going to experience short-term setbacks of 20% or so, though.

This is my ride. It's smoother; I want to sleep better at night. If I can find investments that have lower fees, I can also amp up my returns a bit more without any additional risk.

The third option is the Tea Cup ride. No herky-jerky movements. No need for a seatbelt. Just some relatively smooth sailing. The trade-off is that the returns are likely to be lower.

However, if you have everything else under control, including your spending and your saving habits, this could be a great option for you.

Only you know which ride is best for you.

Chapter 10
An Hour Without Oprah

"Lack of activity destroys the good condition of every human being, while movement and methodical physical exercise save it and preserve it." – Plato

It was one of the more interesting lunch conversations I've had in recent memory.

I was with my colleague Parker at Maggiano's Little Italy in Dallas. Just before tucking into a high-calorie (but classic) meal of salad and Rigatoni D, I told him about some troubling statistics I read the night before.

It turns out that in every state in the U.S., at least *50%* of the residents are either overweight or obese.

Every state! "At least" 50%!

"This is sad," I lamented. But it's more than that. Much more…

It's also the toughest challenge we face as a country. It's not terrorism, trade wars, the makeup of the Supreme Court, violent crime, or any of the bad news we read on a daily basis.

It's a legitimate health crisis, and it's out of control.

In 2010, I bought my own health care insurance for the first time. Initially, the cost was totally manageable, all things considered.

Then, around 2013, insurance rates started to skyrocket.

Insurance companies dropped out of the Texas market.

Coverage worsened, and deductibles grew. When I say "coverage worsened," I'm not exaggerating. But there were only a handful of primary-care providers to cover a million people that lived within miles of Dallas. The doctor I was assigned literally had bars on his windows when I checked out the location on Google Maps.

It was probably *more dangerous* going to the doctor than having any ailments for the doctor to fix.

And, for the privilege, I got to pay more! No, thanks.

By 2017, I was staring down a 100% rise in healthcare... insurance costs. Fortunately, I found a sharing plan that allowed me to cut my monthly premium by about 70%.

I'm lucky. I'm also lucky that I've been healthy.

This Is Inflation

The costs are just out of control.

Of course, anyone can get sick. No matter how prepared you are, you can't protect yourself against everything.

More than 50% of the population is obese or overweight. I understand weight management is a complex issue, with social as well as behavioral variables.

But obesity is, largely, a preventable condition.

Treating illnesses related to it creates enormous costs that – whether we like it or not – silently dominate our culture.

Other quiet health problems plague our system as well.

Anxiety is now No. 3 on the list of most common mental illnesses. It affects 18% of Americans right now, and it's getting worse.

It's hard out there, for young and old alike.

Indeed, we hear about many of these issues – as Parker and I discussed – from Oprah Winfrey.

So many ironies: We're discussing our health routines over massive bowls of pasta, and people are staring at screens to learn how to activate their bodies and minds.

"Imagine an hour *without* Oprah," said Parker.

What folks could do with that hour… a refreshing walk… an invigorating bike ride… a cleaner house…

Millions consume Oprah or other "self-help" media every day.

If they just spend that time getting a little exercise, we might get out of this predicament. Many of us "can't find the time" to exercise. That's often an illusion. We do have the time. It's all about priorities.

Health Equals Wealth

You might wonder what a chapter on taking care of your health has to do with wealth. Here's what…

About one-third of bankruptcies in the United States are health care-related. If premiums are going up 30%, 50%, or even 100% a year, it's only a matter of time before everyone will be bankrupt, save the lucky few.

If you aren't healthy, you aren't wealthy. Today, I live by this philosophy.

I neglected my own health for years. But, after a scare, I started to get serious. These days, I'm getting in an hour of exercise or more nearly every day. It's my top priority.

As I get older, I've focused more and more on my health and what I put into my body. I'm up early in the morning for a high-

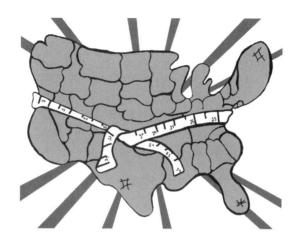

America's growing waistline is costing us a fortune.

intensity bike session, occasional weight-lifting, and time in the sauna. I shed nearly 30 pounds in a matter of months once I got serious. I still have a few more to go.

I'm not a doctor, nor do I play one on TV. So, talk to your doctor about your health and develop a plan so you don't need to visit too often.

But, to give you an idea, here's how my plan came together...

You might say the short story is a "Pitbull" saved my life. But it wasn't a new dog. It was Pitbull the singer/rapper. I'd never heard of him, until one day a song popped up on YouTube. I loved the beat. It was "Hotel Room Service." Great song.

I did a little searching around and found some channels with his greatest hits. I use those songs to amp up my own workouts and work up a sweat. I use a spin bike. I have one at home. It was well worth the investment because spin classes cost a fortune – like $30 a pop. Although the bike wasn't cheap, I got my investment back after just 60 uses. Now it's a free ride, so to speak. I use it practically every day of the week.

When I wake up in the morning, I can't wait to hop on the bike. I admit, I have an addictive personality. Fortunately, I'm putting it to good use. I'm addicted to the bike. When I load up Pitbull's greatest hits, I'm flying.

I also do a dumbbell workout three times a week. I have a set that you can switch out with a few clicks. Makes for an easy workout and supplements my bike rides.

I also have a sauna. That might sound fancy, but I get plenty of "me time" to just relax and meditate. I work up an amazing sweat, and I feel great.

I get some time outside as well. I rekindled my love for snow skiing. It's something I did a lot with my dad when I was a kid. My dad can no longer ski, and, for a while, that bummed me out. Those are great memories. I spent a lot of wonderful times on the slopes with him. More people should ski with their dad. Connections with parents are important. But I also recognize, now, the physical activity part is important too.

I also joined a country club.

Just writing that sentence makes me feel a bit snobby. I'm totally not a country club kinda guy. The good news is that my country club is far different from the Bushwood of "Caddyshack" and all the tropes it represents. There are no snobs. I haven't met one yet.

It's a beautiful place. The course was designed by Jack Nicklaus. It's in immaculate shape. Fortunately, I didn't have to buy into an equity position. That way, when the roof starts leaking, I won't get nailed with an assessment. It's more like a seasonal pass. A reasonably priced one at that. I use the place a lot, so I get a massive return on my investment.

The food is awesome. They don't rip you off, either. The wine program is a steal.

The best part is that I'm treated wonderfully. I'm very much a "please and thank you" person. I'm also a good tipper. Treat service folks well, and you'll be treated like a king.

I joined the country club on doctor's orders. He wanted me to get more exercise. So, I joined to be outside, get a good walk in, and relearn a game that I once loved and was good at. Like I said, I get a lot of use from the club. I like to play in the mornings.

I can play nine holes and be back in the office before the stock market opens. I can walk and play 18 holes in less than three hours.

I learned very quickly to get off the tee not long after sun up. Tuesday morning is senior men's league. They don't play 18 holes in three hours. It's more like a major championship. You'd think there was huge money on the line with the amount of time they take lining up putts! I skip Tuesdays. On Tuesday, I ride the bike.

I practice in the afternoon after the stock market closes. Then, I have a tasty and healthy dinner. I might partake in a glass of wine or my favorite craft beer that they have on tap, and then I head home.

It's eight hours of sleep every night.

Live, Eat, Prosper

And then there's food...

I love to cook. There's nothing better than a big, juicy steak. Ribeye is my favorite. It doesn't need much to melt in your mouth. I love it bloody.

I'm not on the Carnivore Diet, though. I eat plenty of fruits and vegetables. Avocado is my favorite food.

One of the great things about the internet is that it provides a platform for anyone to share ideas and beliefs that otherwise wouldn't get that opportunity in another era. One of the worst things about the internet is that it gives people a platform to share ideas and beliefs.

Nowhere is this more evident than in food. On the internet, there are cult-like followings around certain diets. Vegans will shred you for remotely eyeing a piece of bacon. The carnivores think you're a bozo for eating a ravioli or two. They're deeply entrenched. They can't be swayed to reconsider their beliefs.

I'm not into anything extreme. I have one rule: I don't eat anything that has more than a single ingredient in it.

The other day, I was at Costco Wholesale. There was a low-carb protein drink that was for sale. I looked at the ingredients. There was blue #5 and yellow #3. I remember from kindergarten that "blue + yellow = green." So, it was no surprise that the drink was green.

But there also was something in there called "malic acid." I have no idea what "malic acid" is. I'm also not sure that food coloring is all that great. There was more than one ingredient, so no thanks!

An avocado is an avocado. Fish is fish. An apple is an apple. That's all I need to know.

Do research. Seek knowledge. Avoid the fringes of the internet.

Let's all live long, prosperous lives.

Chapter 11
Unbounded Wealth and the Sonic Jubulator

*"Nature is pleased with simplicity.
And nature is no dummy." – Sir Isaac Newton*

It's time to get down to brass tacks. If you're on the path to financial fitness, the question we now face is where to invest and grow our bankroll.

Today, there are more options than ever before. Heck, there are actually more indexes that track stocks than there are stocks listed on public markets.

You can buy an exchange-traded fund (ETF) that invests in just about anything. For example, there are ETFs that only invest in global carbon, livestock, obesity, and Millennials. That's to name just a few of the obscure.

The problem is, when you slice your investments very thin, it makes it more complex. Like Einstein said, "Everything should be made as simple as possible, but not simpler."

Slicing your investment pie thinly isn't always a good thing. I once tried to slice a cucumber too thin on a very sharp mandolin, and I took three-quarters of the tip of my thumb with it. Your portfolio might get chopped if you buy too many different things.

Don't get too fancy!

Simply Smart

Here's a simple investment strategy Einstein himself would've admired, if, perhaps, only for the name alone. It's called the Sonic Jubulator.

What's a Sonic Jubulator, you ask? I have no idea! I just made up the name. It means *nothing*. But it *sounds* intriguing *and* fancy. As humans, we tend to be attracted to intriguing and fancy.

Filet Mignon is pretty much the same thing as beef tenderloin. But when you call it "Filet Mignon" you're able to charge $5 more per serving! Catch my drift?

So, now that we have a fancy name for our investment strategy, you're more likely to pay attention.

The Sonic Jubulator is an investment strategy rooted in the brilliance of two of the greatest minds of Western Civilization – Sir Isaac Newton and "Iron" Mike Tyson.

Mike Tyson, the former heavyweight boxing champion, is the author of one of my favorite quotes. He once said, "Everyone has a plan until they get punched in the mouth."

Not only is it funny, it's also incredibly insightful. You can go through life with a plan, doing all the right things. But when you (inevitably) get punched in the mouth, you'll go down for the count if you don't know how to respond.

Very simply, in life – especially when it comes to financial markets – we have no idea what the future holds. People make all sorts of predictions about the economy, the stock market, next year's World Series winner… but, in the end, nobody knows anything.

The only people who know – or claim to know – are either lying or slinging bullsh*t.

That doesn't mean these people aren't smart. Smart people love to sound smart. They love to create the impression that they know something others don't. But life is full of left jabs and upper cuts, and the best laid plans are just that. Plans. They are not reality.

As Tyson so profoundly noted, we just don't know what's going to happen. So, part of our investment strategy will deal with that fact of life.

On Motion

Of course, Einstein and his Theory of Relativity changed everything in the 20th century. But, remember, this is about "simple." That's why we're setting aside complex stuff like "relativity" and getting to the roots of physics.

It so happens that Sir Isaac also authored some of the greatest quotes of all time. Here's one: "An object in motion stays in motion until acted on by another force." That happens to be Newton's First Law of Motion.

How does this relate to financial markets? Simple. Financial markets are often defined by trends. A trend occurs, for example, when a stock goes up in price and keeps going up in price… then it goes up in price even more. The fact that it is going up in price may defy logic and gravity.

During my career, I've seen plenty of examples of stocks that have no business going up, up, up, and up. But they do. They may be "overvalued." Their business models might make zero sense.

Back in the 1990s, Pets.com and its sock-puppet mascot reached the stock market equivalent of Mount Everest before it crashed and burned. Who knew a sock puppet could create a billion dollars in value?!

In an uptrend, the price rises. Until it stops rising.

Tyson + Newton = Great Investing Returns

The opposite also happens. Sometimes, stocks go down in price. And they continue to trend into the abyss. It doesn't mean they're bad businesses.

In 2017, while the stock market was reaching new highs, shares of General Electric were taking an absolute beating. General Electric was the last original stock still in the Dow Jones Industrial Average. It's not a fly-by-night operation. They used to "bring good things to life."

GE is as American as hot dogs and apple pie. That doesn't matter. The stock price dropped like a rock.

We can sit around and come up with all sorts of theories why this might be the case. But it's all guesswork. A lot of smart people own GE shares. And – in 2017, anyway – they lost a bundle.

Trends can be self-reinforcing cycles. What's going higher will go higher until it stops going higher. What might cause it to stop going higher? Who knows? Maybe a punch in the mouth.

Nevertheless, an object (share of stock) in motion (going up in price) will stay in motion (keep going up) until acted upon by another force (a punch to the mouth).

Two Truths

Another way to think about it is "the trend is your friend until the end when it bends." We want to identify a trend and ride it like a wave.

We may be able to identify all sorts of reasons why that trend shouldn't occur. The economy is bad. Unemployment is rising. The housing market is tanking. Gas prices are through the roof. Yet, if it's going higher, it's going higher, and there's nothing you can do about it.

But we can make money riding it, surf that wave to profits.

So, the Sonic Jubulator acknowledges two great truths:

- The future is unknowable; be prepared to be punched in the mouth.
- Trends persist in life and in financial markets; ride them to profit.

The Sonic Jubulator divides the portfolio pie into two slices. One half is "Iron" Mike Tyson, the other Sir Isaac Newton.

Within each half, we invest according to the two great truths. In the Tyson half, we prepare for a punch in the mouth. In the Newton half, we surf the market's prevailing trends. The combination works harmoniously to yield respectable investment results.

So, which funds should you use?

Remember: Keep it simple. The big asset classes are stocks, bonds, and commodities.

First, I use the stock market. Specifically, I use the U.S. stock market. You can buy international stocks. But guess what? Major companies in the U.S. do just as much business beyond our borders – if not more – as they do within them.

The most widely used benchmark for the U.S. market is the S&P 500 Index. It was developed and is maintained by S&P Dow Jones Indices, a joint venture with origins dating to the 1880s.

The S&P 500 includes 500 large companies. It's "weighted" based on market capitalization, so the companies with the largest market values make up the bulk of the index.

Where I can, I use the total stock market. This includes thousands of other U.S. stocks. The big companies still make up the bulk of the index, too.

However, introducing even a smattering of smaller companies can, over time, increase your returns a slight but still significant amount. Call it about 0.5% annually. Half a percentage point doesn't sound like much. But – over 30 years – it adds up to a lot of extra dough in your retirement account.

Next, I use bonds. Specifically, I use long-term U.S. Treasury bonds. These bonds are backed by the full faith and credit of the federal government of the United States of America.

Let's take a moment to talk about U.S. government financial products. Now, there are all sort of conspiracy theories that the U.S. is going to hell in a handbasket and that government bonds may someday not be worth the paper they're printed on. After all, Uncle Sam is tens of trillions of dollars in debt. Owning those bonds is risky!

These theorists – I imagine many of whom hoard canned foods in their backyard apocalypse shelters – will remind you of the days of the Weimar Republic, in the aftermath of the First World War, when Germans filled wheelbarrows full with Deutsche Marks just to buy a loaf of bread…

That's great history. What they fail to point out is that the U.S. dollar is *the* currency of the world. If you've been fortunate enough to travel the globe, you'll know that local merchants in faraway places will often accept good old greenbacks before they'll take their home currency.

Still, a funny thing happens when the world does go to hell in a handbasket: People everywhere hoard U.S. dollars! It's a flight to safety. It's like that little blanket you held tightly while you sucked your thumb and wondered how many scary monsters hid in your closet.

In fact, even when the U.S. is in crisis, there's strong demand for the U.S. dollar. Remember 2008? The world teetered on the brink of economic collapse, all because of a subprime lending crisis that started here in America.

On the way to Armageddon, guess what the U.S. dollar did? It went up.

The last asset is gold. Gold is also controversial. Some people love it. Some people hate it. It's been around forever, and it's always had value.

The beauty of these three investments is that they often balance each other out. Stocks might go up while gold is flat. Bonds might rise a little bit. Or any combination. The beauty is that it leads to a smoother ride. Just plop a third of your total investable funds into each of the three asset classes, and you're good to go.

I want to emphasize the importance of a "smooth ride." It's important, because whatever portfolio you invest in, I want you to stick with it!

The goal here isn't to generate the highest possible return. If you seek big numbers, you're best allocating 100% of your funds to stocks. The problem is you run the risk of numerous 50% declines along the way. Most people can't tolerate that.

This portfolio is much easier on the stomach. You won't experience nearly the same level of upset as you would going 100% stocks.

And the results are consistent over time. Let's look at two distinct time periods; we'll go back to the 1970s, and we'll also consider this era of ETF-enabled investing.

Since 1970, the portfolio generated an annual return of 6% *above* inflation. That compares to 7.6% for the total stock market. While the returns are a bit lower than just being in stocks, so is the risk! The biggest hit to your portfolio is 20%. The market? A 49% decline.

Meanwhile, the longest it took Tyson to get back to even after a decline was just five years. Compare that to 14 years for the overall market.

Fourteen years is a long time. Think about it: That's a child's journey from day one of grade school to about halfway through college. It's difficult to sit that long and watch your portfolio try to get back to even.

Let's fast forward to 2004, when there were ETFs available in each asset class to build the portfolio.

Here's what we get. Compared with just owning the total stock market, the returns are 181% for Tyson and 216% for the market. But the "worst beatdown" marks are -21% and -55%, respectively.

See, when the bear market emerged in 2008, not having all your eggs in the stock market basket saved you big time. You just don't know when the next one is coming!

Could you have weathered the storm in 2008? Possibly. Most people didn't. They panicked. And, then, they missed a big opportunity as the market roared back a few months later.

Because most people can't hang on, the longer you stick with the program, the more of your friends and neighbors you'll outperform. Eventually, you're among the top 1% of all investors.

A more conventional 60% stock, 40% bond portfolio earned 138%. But the portfolio still got spanked 35% at its worst.

Now, let's look at the Newton piece. All you do is buy the S&P 500 when it's above its 200-day moving average at the end of a month.

The 200-day moving average is commonly used to determine if price is going up or down. If the market is above the 200-day moving average of its prices, the market is going up. If it's below, it's going down.

What's more, since 1929, when the average is rising the market is up 7.5%. When it's falling, the market is only up 1.7%. That means virtually all the market's gains happen when the average is up! The numbers are a little better in recent times.

According to Sentimentrader.com, since 1970, when the market is above the 200-day moving average, it's up 10%. When it's below the 200-day moving average, it's up 6%. But we don't know if another big crash or two is coming. Actually, we *do* know they *are* coming.... we just don't know *when*.

Famed billionaire investor Paul Tudor Jones teaches an undergraduate course on investing at the University of Virginia. He tells his student he's going to save them the $100,000 tuition to attend business school if they follow a simple rule. You want to be in the direction of the trend, and Paul Tudor Jones uses the 200-day moving average.

It's that simple.

There's nothing new here. Going back to 1971, the annual return for being in the market when it's above the 200-day moving average on a monthly basis is 10.33%. If you bought and held the market, you'd be up almost exactly the same, 10.29%.

However, if you just bought and held, you'd have experienced a massive 51% loss compared to just 23% using the 200-day moving average as a guide.

If you're smart and disciplined, money tends to show up in the places you'd least expect it.

Here are the results from the same start date as the Newton ETF portfolio above... 296% for Newton, 231% for holding the market.

The important point is that Newton suffered a pullback of just 18%. The market? 55%. Ouch.

The Magic

Let's go back to 1970 again. "Raindrops Keep Falling on My Head" is playing on the radio, and "Gunsmoke" is one of the top TV shows in the nation. You decide to plunk $100 in the Sonic Jubulator.

By 2018, the $100 is worth $10,326. Over 100 times your money! Had you invested in just the stock market, you'd have $11,077. Better, not by much.

The magic is that the worst punch in the mouth for the Sonic Jubulator was just 14%. The market got kicked in the pants for 55%. Very similar returns. Much less risk.

One Final Thought

This experiment is just to show you that "simple" works. There are plenty of free resources on the internet to play around with.

A good one is PortfolioCharts.com, a platform that allows you to make up your own portfolio and provides charting tools that help you contextualize losses and answer questions such as, "How long will it take to fund my retirement?"

If you want to look at trends, ETFReplay.com has some basic free stuff on their site.

Don't try to boil the water in the ocean. Keep it simple and consistent, and you'll be rewarded.

Chapter 12

The Show Me The Money Strategy to Crushing the Market in Minutes a Month

"Show me the money!" – Jerry Maguire

If you've watched the movie *Jerry Maguire*, you certainly recognize the title of this chapter and the epigraph introducing it.

I emphasize it because that's the same strategy we want to use when we pick stocks.

It cuts through the danger and makes the process fun. Let's take those two in turn.

If picking individual stocks can be dangerous, why do it at all?

For one, it's a way to really juice your returns. And you don't need to find a lot of big winners. Just a few can make all the difference in the world to your finances.

Meanwhile, it also can be fun to uncover what, in the current market environment, qualifies as "hidden" profit opportunities.

Now, what do I mean by fun and hidden? I'm talking Freddie Prinze Jr. and brick-and-mortar department stores...

You see, this "old school" combination can help make you rich.

Not Just Another Teen Movie

Remember the kinda-classic late 1990s gem *She's All That*?

At the end of the movie, Freddie's big-man-on-campus jock has to choose between his hot, cheerleader girlfriend and Rachel Leigh Cook's nerdy weirdo who he's spent the last month trying to turn into the prom queen to win a bet. He ends up going with the weirdo, and they live happily ever after.

Now, here's what the hell that has to do with investing...

If you had the option to put your money into a hot cheerleader stock – say, Apple – or a nerdy weirdo – like Dillard's – which would you choose?

To a lot of people, the answer seems obvious. But, just like Freddie did at the prom, you should take a closer look at your two choices.

Life with Apple will almost certainly include more excitement. But it wouldn't compare to life with Dillard's.

From the depths of the Global Financial Crisis/Great Recession through 2018, Dillard's stock would've actually made you 449% more than Apple.

Talk about a happy ending... a 1,754% return is good, clean fun.

That said, if the idea of picking stocks scares you or just isn't right for you, you don't need to do it. Investing in exchange-traded funds and then going off to do something you enjoy will be much better for your wealth and health.

If you want the chance to get bigger returns, then let me be your "Ambassador of Quan" for a moment and show you a strategy that thumps the market without a lot of extra work. In fact, just keeping tabs on your positions a few minutes a month is all that's required.

Why "show me the money!"? What does that even mean, anyway?

Well, we want to focus on companies that *pay us* first. This is important because if we're getting paid first, we're reducing some of the risk of owning a stock. Management teams are highly incentivized to keep a stock price up. Their bonuses, stock options, and other forms of compensation depend on it. Their jobs depend on it!

Wall Street is very short-term focused. It's funny, because companies are supposed to have indefinite lifespans. But, for some odd reason, management needs to please Wall Street analysts, bankers, money managers, and other investors *every three months*.

Failure to do so can lead to a stock getting whacked, and hard. Millions – even billions – in value can be lost in minutes. Stocks fall a lot faster than they go up. There's no time to get out of the position before a stock starts tanking on any hint of bad news.

Of course, management teams know this. So, they may resort to playing games with accounting and other shenanigans to keep the stock price up hoping that things get better the next quarter. Or the next quarter after that.

It's a loser's game. We want to play a winner's game. We can do this by getting paid first.

How do we get paid first? There are a few ways.

The most obvious one is a dividend. When companies pay dividends, they're paying cash to you directly out of their coffers. It's simple. You own the stock. Management declares a dividend. You get paid.

Market participants don't seem to focus as much on dividends today as they did in the past. But there's no better indicator of a quality stock than how much it pays its shareholders. Consistent dividend growth can also mean much better performance for your portfolio.

According to Ned Davis Research, companies that initiate and grow dividends have the highest returns since 1972, by nearly 13% annually… with less risk. That's a full percentage point above companies that pay dividends and don't grow them. It's two points better than companies that don't pay dividends. And it's four points higher than companies that cut dividends, which is the kiss of death. Over 47 years, that adds up to a massive difference in your bottom line.

Higher returns with less risk is the holy grail of investing.

The second way to get paid first is when a company buys back stock.

Buying back stock is like a dividend. You don't get paid directly. But management is, hopefully, buying back undervalued shares. That reduces the total number of shares outstanding and boosts earnings per share; if earnings stay the same and shares go down, earnings per share go up…

Of course, not all buybacks are equal. Companies can buy back stock to boost that earnings per share figure even though business is weak. We need to be wary here.

We have a couple good checks to perform to verify companies are on solid enough footing for a buyback program to make sense.

First, they must generate cash flow. Lots of it. Gushing cash flow allows management a lot of financial flexibility. They can increase dividends or buy back stock. They could buy another business, if it makes sense.

By demanding cash flow, you can often bypass a dangerous scenario. That scenario is when a company's cash flow stinks, business is underperforming, and management still takes on more debt to buy back stock and fund the dividend payment. Cut the dividend and you're in the penalty box. For a long time.

The "Titanic" Always Sinks

Together, dividend and buyback activity generate what's called "shareholder yield." But remember: It's not all created equal. It can be deceiving. And it can sink your portfolio.

IBM is an example of bad shareholder yield. Call it the RMS Titanic of the stock market.

There was a time when you could do no wrong buying Big Blue – its products or the company's stock. It was safe for technology purchasing managers to buy from IBM because it was the biggest company in the space. It was the standard to which all software was written and all hardware was built.

Remember the cliché "no one ever got fired buying from IBM"?

That was a good business to have. Then the world changed.

IBM hit the iceberg. The problem is no one knew it, nor that the ship was sinking.

The orchestra's set on the deck is stretching out, folks. Clueless investors have been duped by management, who wasted tens of billions of dollars in capital buying back stock and supporting the dividend as the whole vessel took on water.

A huge problem facing IBM is, back in the old days, when large contracts came up for renewal, nearly 100% of the time the

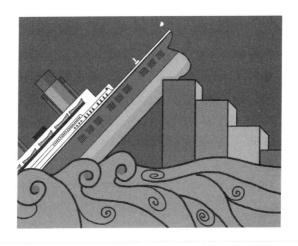

Even sure things can hit an iceberg.

customer renewed the deal with IBM. Often at a higher price. Business was sort of on autopilot.

Times have changed. Competition is fierce. The world is flat. Competitors in India are more competitive. Deals don't get renewed like they used to. Prices are under constant pressure. Growth is slowing. Cash flow is weakening. And IBM can't get back the billions of dollars it wasted to engineer its financial statements.

When IBM gets kicked out of the big indexes, there will be lots of sellers. The next bear market will also likely see threats to the company's dividend. It's no longer a widows-and-orphans stock, either.

Obviously, IBM doesn't score well in our process. While the stock market was hitting new highs, IBM's stock has been stuck in the mud.

The second check is to demand that cash flow is higher than net income.

Why?

You can't spend net income. You can only spend cash flow. Net income is determined by all sorts of accounting-related issues. It's important to understand that there's a lot of leeway for management to make net income look like however they need it to please investors.

Business ebbs and flows. There could be a quarter where net income is higher than cash flow. It's not the end of the world. But, in general, it's good to see cash flow consistently higher than net income quarter after quarter.

If not, there better be a good explanation for why cash flow lagged.

3,200% in 15 Years

Let's talk about debt.

Another step a company can take to create more financial flexibility is to seek cheaper debt. For example, if management swaps high-interest debt for lower-interest debt, there's a savings there. It's not much different than a consumer consolidating credit card debt. (You should be working to eliminate it if you have any.)

Switching from higher interest payments to lower interest payments so that you have more cash in your pocket is simple and smart.

Not all debt is bad. Debt can be an asset if the return on that capital is high enough.

If IBM is the Titanic of wasting capital, perhaps AutoZone is Apollo 11 headed to the Moon... and debt was the rocket fuel.

In the late 1990s, money manager Eddie Lampert started snapping up shares of AutoZone, the auto parts retailer. The beauty of AutoZone is that its business operated with very low start-up and maintenance costs. Its distribution system remains very efficient.

And that means cash flow, lots of it.

Lampert came up with a simple but brilliant idea: Rather than blow the company's wad on ruinous expansion, take a decent business and use the excess cash flow to pay shareholders first!

This is the George Costanza approach to retail. It's the opposite of what others have done. The road to retail riches is paved with the corporate corpses of companies that expanded too rapidly and didn't use cash flow effectively.

Remember Radio Shack? Blockbuster? Boston Chicken?

Lampert had a stable business on his hands, with predictable cash flows. There was more than enough cash to maintain existing stores while opening new ones at a modest pace in strategic locations.

Stable business, steady cash flow, and rolling over into lower-cost debt created enough flexibility for him to buy back 78% of AutoZone's stock. Seventy-eight percent!

While revenues grew 142% and profit margins doubled, earnings per share grew by more than 2,000%.

The result of this "shareholder yield" strategy was a tidy 3,200% gain in 15 years.

Don't Choose Poorly

Making these demands cuts down on candidates for your investment cash. It helps you avoid a lot of glossy, glitzy, or gluttonous hype in the market.

One problem these days – just like during the Internet Bubble – is the number of multi-billion dollar initial public offerings we're seeing. Just like the late 1990s, many of them have no business being publicly traded businesses.

Many of them will crater.

Look at Uber Technologies. It went public with valuation of about $80 billion. And it lost about $2 billion in 2018. There's a lot of risk there. Even if it went to a half a trillion, your returns are about the same we saw in our Dillard's case study.

Meanwhile, you have to make multiple leaps of faith to get there.

Uber bleeds cash. There's no hope of a dividend in sight. Forget any sort of buyback program anytime soon; in fact, I wouldn't be surprised if management issues more stock over the coming years just to keep its business afloat.

It's the exact opposite of what we want to see.

Indeed, we're looking for *undervalued assets*, not overhyped or overpriced fad stocks.

Cash and Pleasure Center

Imagine…

It's a warm summer day… the sun's been beating on your back as you mow the lawn… again…

The darn lawn always seems to need mowing amid the heat of late July, early August… but it's the humidity that gets you. That makes a long, hot mow even longer and even hotter.

There is, of course, a treat waiting for you when that last blade's been sliced. I'm talking more than the sweet, sweet smell of fresh-cut grass… much more…

It's an ice-cold beer. There's nothing better than reaching into the fridge, grabbing a bottle of suds, and cracking it open. I enjoy a cold beer on a hot day after doing chores. Chances are you do, too!

We're not the only ones. In the United States, tens of millions of people consume alcohol on a regular basis. Sometimes, we go a bit overboard. This is actually a global phenomenon with deep historical roots.

Consider the fact that Alexander the Great may have been buried alive because he drank a few pints of wine over the course of a day and a half. His loyal soldiers thought he was dead when he contracted a paralyzing condition. So, they stuck him in the ground. I'm sure the numerous pints of wine didn't help his cause.

Nothing new there. My point is, why not invest in a trend that's been in place for… centuries?

In good times and/or in bad, we want our favorite beverage. In a financial pinch, your favorite tipple and mine is one of the last things we'll cut back. You might stop going out to drink. But you'll still stop by the local package store and bring the goods home to enjoy on the sofa.

There's nothing more durable than that. It's a great defensive play in a volatile stock market. But there's also upside when the economy's humming along.

The Power and the Throne

It's likely you've never heard the name Diageo. If you've ever partaken in a cocktail or two, you've probably sampled their goods.

Would you like your Martini made with Tanqueray or Ketel One? Or do you prefer Diddy's Cîroc?

Diageo has you covered with an all-star line-up of spirits. What's more, they're available everywhere. Its presence is diverse and ubiquitous, and that makes for a massive protective "moat" against competitors.

The case for investing in a company like Diageo is built on brand loyalty, demographics, and strong cash flows. It enjoys solid, consistent growth.

That's because the booze market isn't as mature as major food products, for example. Industry research suggests that the $44 billion industry can grow 6% through 2022. That's a much faster pace than the market for food products, which tends to grow at the same rate the population grows.

Diageo's "premium" actually comes from… "premiumization." That's the process by which a consumer graduates to higher-end

Big money can be made in items we know about, like cocktails.

brands. This results in great dollar value to Diageo because those brands cost more.

This trend bodes well for Diageo. And management is focusing its efforts to maximize its opportunity. The good news is, its efforts to streamline its offerings and emphasize its premium brands have paid off.

Sometimes "smart" is defined by what you stop doing. Diageo exited the wine business in 2015. It might sound romantic to own a vineyard and blend grapes, but it's a tough business.

Personally, apart from owning DEO, I prefer to approach it this way…

When the movie *Sideways* hit theaters, one of the most quoted lines in the movie tanked the demand for what had been a pretty popular varietal. But Paul Giamatti set the price: "I am NOT drinking any f***ing merlot!"

A buddy of mine who worked at Diageo called me up and said when the next "friends and family" wine sale came up to buy as much merlot as I possibly could. He told me they had a warehouse full of it, it was very high-end stuff, and it would be sold for pennies on the dollar.

They had to get rid of it because of Paul Giamatti – a great actor, certainly, but even he couldn't make me buy into his character's depressed tantrum.

I think I bought it for $9 a bottle. A couple years later, I'd see it in stores for $60 a bottle.

The wine business is fickle. Restaurants that change their lineup often look for the best deals. Not always the best wines. There's some loyalty at the high end, but nothing near what you see with spirits.

Meanwhile, Diageo started shedding low-end spirits as well. In November 2018, management sold 19 low-end brands to Sazerac for $551 million and then announced they'd return $441 million to shareholders in the form of a new buyback program.

Paying shareholders first! That's exactly what we want to see! And it makes sense for everybody.

This strategy allows the company to focus on the faster-growing high end of the market. While low-end brands have experienced a declining growth profile, Diageo knows that "people are not drinking less. They are drinking better."

This isn't just CFO-speak. It's showing up in the numbers.

The trend toward higher-end spirits has been in place for at least a few years. In 2017, high-end spirit sales represented 55% of total volume and 62% of total dollar sales. Premium whiskey and tequila sales represent 65% of spirits growth. Meanwhile, mid- and value-priced tiers added only 0.8% to growth in the industry.

Diageo's stock has been a workhorse for *years*. It just grinds along, creating more value. Since the financial crises, the stock is up over 300%. Imagine… 300% for a company whose products you probably use but likely didn't even know their name.

Booze. It's not exactly "sexy" business in a market environment seemingly defined by hope for what artificial intelligence, "big data," and quantum computing can do.

But it is extremely profitable when shareholders come first.

The Show

Here's a quick recap of the "Show Me the Money!" strategy:

- We want to see cash flow. Lots of it.
- Cash flow typically should be higher than net income. We can only spend cash, not earnings.
- Dividends are great. We get paid first. We want the business to be doing OK. No monkey business by management, either.
- Buybacks are very good. If the stock is undervalued and business is OK, they make sense.
- Swapping higher-cost debt for lower-cost debt means savings and higher cash flow.

- A hidden asset could pay us back, hugely. Be on the lookout for assets that management can unload to generate cash to pay us first.

How does it perform?

I invented it in 2009. I've tested it back to 2000. On a "back-test" basis from 2000 through 2018, Show Me the Money! has generated 821% compared with a total return of 147% for the S&P 500 Index.

On a "live" basis since 2009, those numbers are 523% and 243%, respectively.

Those periods have included two market crashes as well as several other mini-scares, including the May 2010 "Flash Crash," the "Brexit" vote in June 2016, and Donald Trump's election in November 2016.

I have charged $25,000, $75,000 and beyond to consult using this software. Hundreds of millions of dollars are managed using my formulas.

But it gets even better. Recently, I made some changes to my approach to narrow the universe to high yielding stocks first. Then I run it through the meat grinder to make the sausage. You see, today interest rates are getting cut. Those lower rates are going to rob you of trillions of dollars in savings.

You think mobsters and drug dealers are hardened criminals? They're nothing compared with central bankers. Those are the real thieves. Those bankers are going to rob you of trillions of dollars in savings yet no one is going to go to jail.

If you can predict whether a company is going to raise its dividend, you have a huge edge. Of course, nothing is certain 100% of the time. But, it's certain enough.

That edge has generated returns in excess of 4,000% since 2000 based on the testing I have done. Just a few tweaks amped the returns five times over!

The cream always rises to the top. By focusing on shareholder friendliness while sprinkling in a mix of factors that took 20,000 hours of work to think about and develop, a sound plan was put in place.

Remember, this is *your* hard-earned money.

Investing in financial markets isn't buying a lottery ticket. Demand quality. Demand that management pay your first.

Do that, and, over time, you'll be rewarded.

Epilogue
Just 12 Simple Steps

Now we are at the end of our journey. Just 12 simple steps. Follow them and you'll start to get ahead. Over time, you'll get further ahead. After more time you'll be so far ahead that the world will be your oyster.

To break free of "The Man" may require some sacrifice. There's no get rich quick scheme. The average person isn't taking advantage of even some of the easiest ways to make money such as contributing to your 401(k). It's free! What's better than free money?

Take care of the basic principles and you can still enjoy life. You like that $5 cup of coffee? Great, if it makes your life better, go for it. As long as you take care of business up front. You know, if you buy a great coffee maker and make it at home instead, your payback is just a couple of months. Simply stashing the difference in the daily coffee habit can yield hundreds of thousands of dollars in more savings during your golden years.

For my 40th birthday I went to Beverly Hills. I stayed at the same hotel as Julia Roberts in Pretty Woman. I ate my birthday dinner at a famous restaurant called Spago, helmed by world-renowned chef Wolfgang Puck.

It was an experience I'll never forget. Here's the thing: I was able to do that because for years I had been following the principles in this book. Instead of buying some shiny object I'd soon lose interest in, I created a wonderful memory for life.

That's not my day-to-day life. I don't hang out in Beverly Hills on a regular basis. In fact, I haven't been back since.

Most of the things I enjoy in life are low cost. I get so much joy going for a hike with my little dog. The cost? Virtually nothing. It's whatever it costs in gas to get there.

Yes, there will be some sacrifice. Especially if you have to dig out of a debt hole. Life can still be enjoyed, too.

It's the best of both worlds. The freedom to do what you want when you want. Only you can make it happen!

It's time to get started!

Other Works from John Del Vecchio

Rule of 72: How to Compound Your Money and Uncover Hidden Stock Profits

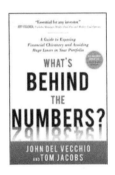

What's Behind the Numbers? A Guide to Exposing Financial Chicanery and Avoiding Huge Losses in Your Portfolio.

For more information on these books, as well as how you can begin receiving actionable trading opportunities from John Del Vecchio's premium research services, please visit www.unboundedwealth.com.